D1642246

THE BOOK OF THE DUN COW

Walter Wangerin, Jr.

Allen Lane

ALLEN LANE
Penguin Books Ltd
17 Grosvenor Gardens
London SW1 0BD

First published in the U.S.A. by Harper & Row,
Publishers, Inc., and simultaneously in Canada
by Fitzhenry & Whiteside Limited, 1978
First published in Great Britain by Allen Lane 1980
Copyright © Walter M. Wangerin, Jr., 1978

ISBN 0 7139 1328 2

Printed in Great Britain by
Richard Clay (The Chaucer Press) Ltd
Bungay, Suffolk

Talitha, Mary, Matthew, and Joseph appear in this story, each a separate character. And Thanne is here, too—both the woman and her quiet love.

To these this book is dedicated.

TABLE OF CONTENTS

PART TWO

PART THREE

[ix]

PART ONE

[ONE] *How Mundo Cani came to live with Chauntecleer*

n the middle of the night somebody began to cry outside of Chauntecleer's Coop. If it had been but a few sprinkled tears with nothing more than a moan or two, Chauntecleer would probably not have minded. But this crying was more than a gentle moan. By each dark hour of the night it grew. It became a decided wail, and after that it became a definite howl. And howling—particularly at the door of his Coop, and in the middle of the night—howling Chauntecleer minded very much.

Chauntecleer the Rooster had trouble sleeping anyway, though this was no one's fault but his own. He snored. Well, Chauntecleer *called* it a snore, and everybody else who lived in his Coop called it a snore, too. But everybody else knew secretly that it was a positive crow.

This is the way that it went: As dusk fell, the whole company of the Coop would take to their roosts, tuck their heads deep into their neck and shoulder feathers, ruffle, cluck, and fall asleep—Chauntecleer among them. For the space of several hours, silence and contentment would fill the Coop, and sleep was good. But then Chauntecleer would begin to dream; and with his dream he would set up such a sudden, loud, and raucous snoring that every living soul in the neighborhood of the Coop would wake up. Immediately they all had a job to do. They had to pretend that they were still asleep, because it was *Chauntecleer's* snore, after all.

When his snores came close to the sound of thunder,

then Chauntecleer woke up, too. With a headache. And he wouldn't pretend: He was awake, and he was angry about it. He'd cock his eye angrily at this creature and that, looking for guilt, waiting until one poor soul couldn't stand it any longer—and moved!

"You!" Chauntecleer would cry, and the Hen would wilt, moving very much all of a sudden. "Ah-*ha*-ha! You!" The Rooster's comb would stand up like a fan on the top of his head. He would flut down and strut up to the sad Hen and fix her with a one-eyed stare from the side of his rooster head.

"You! You! You! Sleep on my straw. Eat my grain. Hide from the wind, and dry from the rain. And how do you repay my great goodness to you? YOU WOKE ME! How do you like that? And what's more, you woke me *UP!*"

Then Chauntecleer would make a noise which he considered to be something better than a snore. It was a true crow; and it entered the shivering Hen's ear with such a force that she wouldn't sleep for the rest of the night. Back to his perch the Rooster would grump, twisting and turning and mumbling his perturbation: He did most certainly despise to be awakened from his dreams. But finally he would nod and dream again.

It was more than a fact that Chauntecleer the Rooster had trouble sleeping. It was also a well-known fact. All the Coop had a healthy fear of awakening his feathered thunder. Therefore, when someone began to weep outside of his Coop one night, everybody heard it, but nobody moved. And when weeping became wailing, they pretended with a skill both admirable and desperate. And when wailing developed into pure howling, why, every last Chicken turned into a stone.

Oh, their *hearts* were moved. Who wouldn't be moved to pity by that sad, sad voice? Who wouldn't let a tear roll down her beak to hear of the grief which this voice had to tell? All the world seemed a lonely place at the sound of this voice, it wept so pitifully. This voice could make even the stones to cry—which became a particular problem for some thirty Chickens who were trying hard to *be* stones.

"Marooned," he cried, whoever he was out there. "Maroooooned," he wailed. Three stones sniffed, and sixty eyes shot frightened glances at Chauntecleer; but the Rooster slept on.

The voice sounded like ancient shoe leather.

"Don't listen to me," he cried out. "Every good heart should sleep on. No one should be troubled with the burdens which it is given me to bear. Sleep!" he sighed. "Sleep on, peaceful souls!" he wailed. And then he howled: "Maroooooooooooned!"

A little dribble hung down from Chauntecleer's beak, a wet string which went from the tip of his beak to the bottom of his wattle. This was a good sign. It meant that he was sleeping very deeply, and perhaps the Chickens would be safe. Yet no sign was absolute; and this was a most unusual occurrence, this voice abroad; so the Chickens continued to pretend and to fear.

The voice sounded like a mud slide.

"Ah, me! What I could have been in a better place. Such a wonderful somebody I should have been," he wept, "that it would have been a pleasure to look at. But this is the place, and this is the me. Look at me, and be sad. See me and be sorrowful. No!" he wailed suddenly. "No, *don't* look! No one should be burdened with such a sight—a walking sin. But sleep," he wailed. "Sleep and be what I can never be. It does my soul good to know that someone is at peace. Sleep." And then he howled like the north wind: "Maroooooooooned!"

Chauntecleer stirred. He pulled one claw off the perch. Two Chickens fainted; but it was just motion in his sleep. Restless sleep, now; but sleep all the same.

"And what about this nose?" cried the voice outside, wounded deeply by this new sorrow. "All of you, count yourselves blessed. Go home and call yourselves fortunate before the mirror! For if you wish, you can turn your eyes and look away from this monster of a nose. But me?"

"You," said Chauntecleer in his sleep. Another Chicken passed out.

"Ah, Master of the Universe—me!"

"You," drooled Chauntecleer.

"*I* have to look at this nose all the time, for here it sits between my eyes. Between my eyes, like a boot all the day long. Every time I look at anything, there is my nose underneath it. Ah, me, me! But you—sleep on forever. Sleep! Sleep!" Then came the cry like a gunshot: "*Sleep!*"

Chauntecleer woke up so fast that he swallowed his spit and gagged.

"Hear it," howled the voice outside at the top of his lungs. "I am a walking sorrow. To look at me is to break your heart; but here is my nose and I can look on nothing else but me. Marooned! Marooned in this sad excuse of a body. Maroooooooned!"

That did it.

Chauntecleer had been snapping his head left and right to prove to himself that there really was a sound about. For a moment he had been so astonished by the noise that he thought it a leftover dream. Who would be such a fool as to make such a noise? Yet there was that word coming down out of the air like an avalanche: "Marooned!" as real as his headache. That's what did it.

Chauntecleer the Rooster began to beat his wings. "Cock-a, cock-a," he started to say, but that wasn't loud enough, not nearly furious enough. He threw out his chest; his neck feathers bristled: "Cock-a-doodle, cock-a-doodle," and still that wasn't what he wanted. It should have some cursing in it.

He jiggled up and down on the perch, bent his head so far backward that it touched his tail feathers, and cried: "Cock-a-MAMIE! Cock-a-cock-a-BULL! COCK-A-DOO-DLE-DOO!"

[6]

That was what he wanted.

But it was almost as if the voice outside were happy to hear what Chauntecleer had to say, for the word came back with something like a note of conversational cheer in it: "MAROOONED!"

Chauntecleer was stunned. Seven Chickens fainted dead away. But Chauntecleer didn't notice the bodies falling off their perches. He did something else.

It must be understood that Chauntecleer, though he was able, seldom flew. It was his custom to strut. Strutting permitted pride and a certain show of authority, whereas flying looked mostly foolish in a Rooster: lumpish, graceless and altogether unnecessary. Wings on a Rooster, so Chauntecleer thought, were not for flying. They were for doing absolutely nothing with; for it is a mark of superiority when part of the body does nothing at all. But sometimes Chauntecleer forgot his opinions.

In a white rage he leaped from his perch and beat the air. He flew straight out of the Coop, through the door, and over a Dog.

He saw the Dog as he passed over it. That glance fouled up his landing. He thumped like baggage to the ground and rolled over twice. Feathers exploded.

While Chauntecleer scrambled to stand up amid the feathers, the Dog walked up to him and shed tears on his wing.

"Feathers," wept the Dog. "Soft, wonderful feathers," he said miserably, "which sprout the same as hair. Ah, me," he wept, "mine is only hide. Hide itches at noontime." He laid a sad paw on Chauntecleer's wing.

Chauntecleer hopped backward from this apparition, staring at him, offended and confounded at once. But the Rooster considered himself equal to any occasion. Therefore he split the night air with a ringing crow aimed directly into the Dog's enormous nose. Immediately the Dog fell down in a heap and rolled over on his back.

For a fleeting moment Chauntecleer was satisfied.

[7]

"Hear it," the Dog wept from the bottom of his soul, shaking uncontrollably. "Master of the Universe, listen to this. To one you give such sweet melody; to another you give a growl." His nose ran like a river. "Marooned," he blubbered.

Chauntecleer did something like a sneeze, but not a sneeze at all. It was anger choking in his throat.

Well, if the first one didn't work, then he thought to try another crow, more commanding even than the last, as powerful as a thunderclap, and so full of purple cursing that this boxcar would get up and gallop away. So he leaped up onto the very chest of the Dog, breathed deeply, and opened his beak next to the flap which he took for an ear.

"COCK-A-BLOODY-IMBECILE!" The crow was tormenting and wonderful. The forest whispered its fear. The leaves shivered.

But the Dog on his back looked up and kissed Chauntecleer on his beak.

"Accept my thanks, thou great heart," he wept softly. "More you have done for me with this one song than my mother in all of her sorrowful life."

Chauntecleer's head snapped back like the cock on a pistol. He was silent for one deadly minute, standing on a roost which was the chest of a Dog. Then the words burst out of him like bullets.

"I have a perch," he cried. "It's warm because I was sleeping on it. I have a Coop. It was quiet for my sleep. A warm perch!" He scratched the Dog's chest with his right claw, as if scratching dirt. "A quiet Coop!" He scratched with the left. "But you, you rug! You sack! YOU WOKE ME UP!"

"Excuse me," whispered the Dog, "for speaking at a time like this, but be kind to yourself as you have been to me—and look in another place."

Chauntecleer lost his speech. Beak open, eye smoking, he stared at the Dog.

[8]

"Look at the skies," whispered the Dog kindly. "Look at the trees where God made beauty. But it is only a sorrow to look on me where God planted ugliness. Ah," sighed the Dog, "such a fine small beak you have."

Not his most piercing, his most murderous crow could move this remarkable rag. Not the words of his anger could send this Dog away. Chauntecleer shuddered with rage. His wattles trembled. His feathers stood out and shivered. And seeing that there was nothing else to do, he bit the Dog savagely, on the nose.

"Amen! I agree with you," the Dog wailed with fresh sorrow. "It is my lasting grief; and I should be grateful if you would bite it off altogether."

"Cock, cock, cock," Chauntecleer choked; and he set to pecking the great nose in front of him as if it were a piano, ripping up hair and taking away bits of skin.

With every peck the Dog said, "Thanks." With every other peck he wept, "But it won't work." And with every third peck he wailed, "Yet thou art more than a friend to me."

There came the time, finally, when Chauntecleer the Rooster himself broke down. After the Dog had begun to croon, "My friend is a surgeon, a doctor sent from heaven with healing in his beak," it happened that Chauntecleer himself began to cry. He slid down to the ground and lay on his back with his two claws pointing up to heaven and gurgled a broken crow. He wept.

And, of course, side by side, each on his back, they made a chorus; for the Dog wept with him.

"It is," said the Dog in commiseration, "a convincing argument, this body. Mountains last forever, though it was a worthy effort, good friend. But mountains last forever, and many a worthy spirit breaks upon them." He sighed, and then wept quietly and almost peacefully.

Suddenly the Rooster said, "Headache. Head*ache!*" he snapped. And then he didn't strut. He stumbled into the Coop.

[9]

The Dog rolled his eyes without rolling his body from its back. "A doctor sent from heaven," he said.

In the morning Chauntecleer the Rooster stepped out of his Coop to crow at the sun and to rouse up all of his Chickens. When he was done, on this particular morning, he coughed hoarsely; and then he noticed that he was standing on something warm. He looked down and saw a Dog smiling up at him. The Dog was shaking his head. There were tears in his eyes.

"Such a voice in such a fine small beak," he said.

"Such a headache," said the Rooster, "from such a rug."

Humbly the Dog lowered his head. "Thank you, Doctor," he said.

The Rooster hopped down and strutted away. His tail feathers were flags behind him. "The name is Chauntecleer," he said, "you doormat."

"It's a little thing; a nothing, really," called the Dog behind him, "but there is a name for me, too. Of course there is no beauty in it. If the Doctor wants to call me Doormat instead of Mundo Cani Dog, this Dog will be happy."

From that day forward, Mundo Cani Dog would feel sad if Chauntecleer crowed to the rising sun from anywhere else but from his own sad and lumpy back.

[two] *Three words about Chauntecleer's ability to crow*

C hauntecleer the Rooster crowed when he was angry, to be sure. Upset, or out of humor, he could crow the fear of God into a wood tick or into nearly anything else, for that matter. But no one must get the idea that this was the only time when he crowed, nor the only kind of crow he knew. Crowing was his profession.

Generally, Chauntecleer divided his crows into two major categories. Certain of them he called his "occasional crows": crows born of the moment, the occasion, the mood, and not according to any due time. Hereunder he had crows for all moods and feelings.

Crows for laughter and crows for grief; a whooping crow for joy, which made joy come alive and dance right there in the Coop; a soft, insinuating crow for shame, at which the Hens would hide their heads under their wings. He could crow a certain spilling crow when he admired something very much. He could warn the stars themselves with a crow like a bloody alarum, and then the stars themselves would stand on guard. And at the death of someone beloved, Chauntecleer the Rooster mourned the passing by strutting to the roof of his Coop and there sounding a throaty crow which rolled across the countryside like the tolling of a heavy iron bell; and then God's creatures would surely pause, bend their heads, and weep.

Crows of pride and crows of glory; crows on the occasion of a victory or a defeat. And crows, too, for the plain sake of crowing.

[11]

But there was another whole set of crows which he used always at certain special hours during the day. These *did* come in due time; and these were called the "canonical crows." They told all the world—at least that section of the world over which he was Lord—what time it was, and they blessed the moment in the ears of the hearer. By what blessing? By making the day, and that moment of the day, familiar; by giving it direction and meaning and a proper soul. For the creatures expected his canonical crows, and were put at peace when they heard them. "Yes, yes," they would say, "the day is our day, because Chauntecleer has made it ours." That they would say in the morning, grateful that by his crow the day should hold no strangeness nor fear for them. And at noon: "The day's halfways over; the best part is still coming." It was a comfort to be able to measure the day and the work in it.

Seven times a day, dutifully, with a deep sense of their importance, and by the immemorial command of the Divine, Chauntecleer crowed his canonical crows.

At dawn, from Mundo Cani's lumpy back, he crowed a fresh, green crow which sounded like chilly water and which awakened the Hens on the spot. When it was time to go to work, he crowed another crow: "A-choo-choo-choo!"—something like a steam engine starting up; and then one couldn't help it; one's wings began to beat and claws would start to scratch the ground, digging for seeds and grubs, and beaks would begin to peck.

At nine o'clock, at noon, and then again at three o'clock the Rooster crowed crows to announce what kind of day was going by. Up went his head, with its comb as red as coral, its beak as black as jet. He listened to the wind; he saw the color of the sky; he watched the scratchers scratching; he considered all the news of all the things which were happening in that day up until that moment—and then he crowed some busy crows about this and that and such and such. Every creature knew the day when Chauntecleer was done with these crows: at nine o'clock, at noon, and then again at three. And kindly did the time pass by.

The sixth crow came when the sun was going down. A Hen was glad to hear it for several reasons. For one, it sounded something like a compliment; it came across the evening air and patted each one on the back, and it made each forehead cool as if with a breeze: "Good," it said. "Good and better than you did yesterday. Now, stop. Eat supper. And rest easy." And so these were the other reasons a Hen was glad to hear it: Work was done and supper was coming.

But the seventh was the kindest crow of all. This was as quiet as nightfall. This crow was the night at peace upon her nest. This was settle, and rest, and "You are safe," and amen, and "Go, now, to sleep." For "Done," when it is well done, is a very good word.

When Chauntecleer crowed his canonical crows, the day wore the right kind of clothes; his Hens lived and scratched in peace, happy with what was, and unafraid of what was to be; even wrong things were made right, and the grey things were explained.

A third word concerning Chauntecleer's crows must now be spoken, though he himself was unaware of it. A third category of crows would, within a year of Mundo Cani's coming to the Coop, burst from Chauntecleer's throat with a terrible power. For an enemy was gathering himself against this Rooster and his land. Within the year Chauntecleer would find his land under a treacherous attack; and then, in that war, this third kind of crowing would become his necessary weapon. Cruel crows; sharp, explosive crows, murderous and thwarting, they would be called "Crows Potens." But Chauntecleer knew nothing of this now: of neither the enemy, nor the war which was to be, nor the killing crows which he had it in him to crow, the "Potens."

For the time being Chauntecleer was busy about lesser affairs, though he himself would have called them important enough.

[13]

[CHREE] Things begin to happen—
treachery is discovered within
the Coop

s he saw it, Chauntecleer did not ask much in return for his constant, abiding, and well-intentioned leadership. Good dinners. Loyalty. A little color in his life. Sleep: unbroken sleep, to be sure. And a morning sunbath, undisturbed. As matters would have it, that sunbath was, once in a while, disturbed.

One morning, several weeks after the appearance of a Dog who carried his baggage in front of his face, Chauntecleer the Rooster was strutting in front of his Coop, enjoying the bright sunlight and the day which went with it. Minor clucks in his throat announced his good pleasure. He had fluffed out his golden feathers so that the sun could shine down to the skin and warm it. His wings were ruffled and loose at his sides. And lazily he went scratching about in search of a proper dry sink of dust into which he would settle, nestle, and rest. This was the sweet progress of his sunbath; he had a dreamy smile on his face.

But suddenly someone in the Coop behind him began to gabble a whole series of despairing clucks. All the other clucks went quiet while that one cry stuttered on with a true pain in it; and then it, too, fell silent, and the Coop was still. And that was wrong. An early morning Coop is almost never silent.

Chauntecleer was irritated. His pleasure had lost its rhythm, and he knew by the silence behind him that he was about to be involved. Yet, for a certain spite, he would not turn around and face the door of the Coop, but continued with the motions of his sunbath, though the spirit of the thing had gone out of it.

Presently a Hen came out and stood behind him. Her name was Beryl. She pecked the ground awhile, as if this were what she always did at this time of the morning behind the Rooster of the Coop. But soon her pecking turned to sighing, and her sighing to little explosions. "Ahhh," she said. "Ohhh," she moaned; and the problem for Chauntecleer was that there was real anguish in her moaning.

So Chauntecleer said, away to the day: "What is it?"

"If it pleases you, sir," Beryl said, and Chauntecleer was irritated the more.

"Sir" and "pleases you" are right and proper things to say to a Lord, of course. But they are also hindrances to clear speech: They keep someone, if there are enough of them, from ever getting to her point. They keep a certain lonely distance between the Lord and his subject. And they keep that Lord too long from his sunbath.

"If it pleases me, sir, *what*?" Chauntecleer said to the day.

"Well, and then I wish it hadn't happened," said Beryl, "but it did happen, and there we are." She sighed wretchedly.

"What happened?" Chauntecleer demanded.

"You can be sure that we didn't wish it, sir. Often we've prayed against the thing. Already at the first time we trembled with pain," she said, and a whole volley of little clucks came out of the Coop, which were as much as to say, "Yes, yes. We were pained about it even then." Beryl took courage from those clucks: "The second time was yet worse, you see," she said.

Chauntecleer decided that he had better turn around. He did, and he eyed the Hen: "*What* was worse, Beryl?"

His full face, his eye, and her name in his mouth made

Beryl timid again. "Oh, well, nothing, really, my Lord. Except that we can't do much about it, though heaven knows we've made the effort." She was looking at the ground.

"About *what*?" the Rooster shouted.

"The eggs," she said quickly.

"Ah," said Chauntecleer. "The eggs."

Beryl curtsied. "Right glad I am, sir, that you understand about the eggs."

Chauntecleer made his black beak to smile. "But you see, little Beryl"—he smiled dreadfully—"I don't understand about the eggs at all, which leaves it up to you to tell me about the eggs." Lordship is always easier in the ordering than in the listening.

"Oh," she said. "Well, they're missing. But then they haven't been missing either, sir." She paused, as if this meant something dolorous to the Rooster. He pretended that it did and shook his head a few times so that she wouldn't stop now.

"My meaning is, sir, that the shell is always still there, broken into pieces. And the good inside of the egg is gone. Eaten. Gone." And Beryl clucked miserable clucks, while several chickens in the Coop clucked with her. Tears glistened in her eyes.

"You can be sure that they were eaten?" Chauntecleer was suddenly altogether serious. Eggs could become children. But not if they were eaten first.

"Licked," Beryl managed to say, "clean."

Chauntecleer was silent for a moment. The moment stretched into minutes, so that Beryl became uneasy; and still the Rooster was bleakly still—coiled.

"If it pleases you, sir," Beryl said full quietly, "then would you crow a crow for me? Sir, the crow of grief?" She was able to look him in the eye when she said this, for a sorrow spoken lends a little courage to the speaker.

But Chauntecleer had something else on his mind, and

[16]

he did not answer her. Instead he gazed at her with blank eyes. And then he stretched his wings and leaped to the top of the Coop, leaving her behind. He looked to the woods nearby and stared at one place only—at a small heap of earth which was at the base of a certain maple tree.

"John Wesley!" he cried out fiercely, suddenly, never moving his eyes from that heap of earth. "John, yo! Wesley, yo! Weasel!" he cried again, but nothing moved. In fact, the heap did such a good job of not moving that it seemed to move in order to keep so still. "John Wesley Weasel!" Chauntecleer cried for the third time.

Then a lonesome voice arose from behind the Coop: "But then again," it mumbled, "if the Doctor thinks up a better name for me, and if he supposes that Weasel is a better title for this sorrowful nose than Doormat, why, that is acceptable. Ugliness has little enough to say in this world. I am no Weasel. I *think* that I am no Weasel. I was a Dog, once. But, considering the matter for a second time, and hearing the Doctor's sweet proclamation . . ."

"Oh, you mournful lummox!" Chauntecleer shouted down at Mundo Cani Dog. "Get up on your legs. Do something!"

"Lummox," said Mundo Cani, arising, "is a great kindness, too."

"John Wesley Weasel lives under that maple," cried the Rooster, pointing. "Bring him to me."

Mundo Cani ambled over to the woods, talking to himself all the way. The heap of earth grew to be even more still, if that is possible. When the dog arrived, though still mumbling, he displayed a sudden and astonishing speed. His paws dug, and the dirt flew out between his hind legs like a brown fountain. Amid the dirt there whirled a furry varmint, which spun for a second in the air and then was snapped into the dog's jaws before it hit the ground.

So then there were two creatures talking as the Dog ambled back to the Coop, both of them incomprehensi-

[17]

ble. One mumbled sadly to himself about this name and the other, testing which one fit his long countenance the best. This he could do even with fur in his mouth. The other squeaked a hundred words per second, all of them protests and denials.

When they came to the Coop, Chauntecleer shouted, "Shut up!" and they did. Except that Mundo Cani first said, "Mmf clmf," which was to say: "It is a kindness that you ask me to do this thing for you. Should I, perhaps, bite his head off?" But as nobody understood him, the Rooster didn't answer one thing and the Weasel didn't answer another.

"Beryl, get the shells," Chauntecleer commanded, still lofty on top of the Coop. While she did, he turned to the Weasel hanging out of Mundo Cani's mouth.

"John Wesley—" he began, but the Weasel didn't wait for a question or a finish.

"Not John!" he chattered. "Nor not John Double-u of the Double-u's neither. Look in other places. Other haunts and hollows. Flip rocks. Root roots. Shake trees. Find a villain. But John Double-u—he's no villain. He didn't do it!" The Weasel's heart was beating so fast that Mundo Cani's eyes jumped.

"Do what?" said the Rooster.

"It! *It*!" the Weasel cried. "The what that put John's little body in a monster's mouth. Whatever. The Rooster knows. This Weasel doesn't. Oh, tell a Dog to put me down. John's wet, he is."

At that moment Beryl came out of the Coop with the empty shells and with grief in her eyes. John Wesley saw her and was silenced.

"John Wesley," Chauntecleer said, "look at those shells."

"Shells," said the Weasel miserably. "Are most certainly shells."

"And empty," said the Rooster.

"Empty," said the Weasel, suddenly of very few words. He knew the tragic importance of eggs eaten out. He knew the loss of children; for one greater than he had taught him. "This is the what," he moaned.

"I know what you have done in the past, John Wesley," said that one. "I know what you are capable of doing."

The Weasel stiffened abruptly. Mundo Cani gagged. "Past is past. Past is not present. Did is not do. Was is not is," chattered John Wesley again, desperate. "This! Oh, not John."

Chauntecleer stared at the Weasel for some moments and considered. Then, with a dreadful measure, he said quietly: "If this isn't your work, John Wesley; if we don't fault you for swallowing children even before they are formed, then whose *is* the fault? Name a name before me, John."

The Weasel closed his eyes and answered nothing. He shivered.

"Mf rmfl," said Mundo Cani—awoken, perhaps, by the shiver. He meant: "One should supper on such a wickedness and be done."

But Chauntecleer cut the silence with a crow and a command:

"A name, John Wesley! It was one or another who's been eating children. One I have here for the punishment. Another's name I do not know. Then: Unless I am given a name, John Wesley, it shall be *you!*"

"Um," squeaked the Weasel in a tiny voice. His eyes opened and tried to see every corner and every hiding place around him.

"A NAME!" roared the Rooster.

"Nezer," squeaked the Weasel hastily.

"Ebenezer Rat?"

Then the Weasel stood up for himself, the name having been said, as best as one might stand up for oneself in the mouth of a Dog: "Rats is rats, past, present, and forever," he chattered. "Weasels change. But rats is rats!"

"Ebenezer Rat," the Rooster pronounced the name blackly.

Suddenly there was an explosion in the Coop, and thirty Hens burst out the door all at one time. They had heard the name.

The commotion caused Mundo Cani to turn circles and to open his mouth. A wet Weasel fell to the ground. Hens spluttered all over the yard, while the Weasel tested his legs and flung sharp glances at a Dog.

"Is *ways* to bite a Weasel," he mumbled. "Is ways to bite a Dog, too."

Mundo Cani, however, had burst into tears. "White loveliness," he wept, pawing Hen after Hen. "Loveliness of white. How is it, Master of the Universe, that you set such grace among the Chickens but to me you give a brown curse for a hide?"

But the compliment was lost on the Hens, who shot about in panic.

"Cock-a-stop!" Chauntecleer crowed from the top of the roof. "Cock-a-lorum! Cock-a-silence! COCK-A-RUD-DY-SHUT-IT-OFF!"

And they did. They all fell silent. All except Mundo Cani, who had a white feather between his paws and the sniffles in his nose.

In the quiet, first one Hen and then one other walked to special places in the yard and scratched at the soft earth. Little holes were made. Chalcedony took something from her hole and brought it below Chauntecleer. She laid it, with great care, upon the ground. Jacinth did the same; and the things which they laid below him were pieces of empty eggshell.

"If it pleases you," they clucked each a lowly cluck to him, "a crow for the grief of these?"

Chauntecleer heard them. He would do this thing for them.

[20]

The morning had turned into a lasting irritation. The night to come, Chauntecleer could foresee, would be without sleep; and so it would be an irritation, too. And there was a plan to be formed in the time between. Irritation. But the plan was necessary, if they were going to do anything about the cruelty of Ebenezer Rat. Chauntecleer sighed. He had seen something fixed in the dry yolk on a piece of Jacinth's shell, a whisker, black, sharp, and exceedingly long. A Rat's whisker. Ah, Nezer, the Rooster sighed; for John Wesley Weasel had been right. And something would have to be done tonight.

But for the present moment . . .

Into the silence—with Beryl, Chalcedony, and Jacinth standing close below him—Chauntecleer lifted up his voice and crowed. And even John Wesley Weasel forgot himself for the moment and listened.

The Coop was empty. Someone took advantage of its emptiness. A small hole existed between two floorboards. Through that hole there slipped a silent, long, long, black nose, and after that a head like a finger pointing: eyes as narrow as needles; a body like black liquid; a tail which came and came and never ceased to slide out of the hole. Dark, smooth, and as quiet as this one was, yet he was no mere shadow.

While the crow of grief rolled out over the countryside, Ebenezer Rat crushed and swallowed one more egg.

[FOUR] *A cosmography, in which Wyrm is described, and one or two things about him*

n those days, when the animals could both speak and understand speech, the world was round, as it is today. It encountered the four seasons, endured night, rejoiced in the day, offered waking and sleeping, hurt, anger, love, and peace to all of the creatures who dwelt upon it—as it does today. Birth happened, lives were lived out upon the face of it, and then death followed. These things were no different from the way they are today. But yet some things were very different.

For in those days the earth was still fixed in the absolute center of the universe. It had not yet been cracked loose from that holy place, to be sent whirling—wild, helpless, and ignorant—among the blind stars. And the sun still traveled around the moored earth, so that days and nights belonged to the earth and to the creatures thereon, not to a ball of silent fire. The clouds were still considered to flow at a very great height, halfway between the moon and the waters below; and God still chose to walk among the clouds, striding, like a man who strides through his garden in the sweet evening.

Many tens of thousands of creatures lived on this still, unmoving earth. These were the animals, Chauntecleer among them, whom God noticed in his passage above. And the glory of it was that they were there for a purpose. To be sure, very few of them recognized the full importance of their being, and of their being *there*; and that ignorance endangered terribly the good fulfillment of their purpose. But so God let it be; he did not choose to force knowledge upon the animals.

What purpose? Simply, the animals were the Keepers. The watchers, the guards. They were the last protection against an almighty evil which, should it pass them, would burst bloody into the universe and smash into chaos and sorrow everything that had been made both orderly and good. The stars would be no help against him; and even the angels, the messengers of God—even the Dun Cow herself—would only grieve before him and then die; for messengers can speak, but they cannot *do* as the animals could.

The earth had a face, then: smiling blue and green and gold and gentle, or frowning in furious gouts of black thunder. But it was a *face*, and that's where the animals lived, on the surface of it. But under that surface, in its guts, the earth was a prison. Only one creature lived inside of the earth, then, because God had damned him there. He was the evil the animals kept. His name was Wyrm.

Deep, deep under the oceans and the continents, under the mountains and under the river which ran from them to Chauntecleer's land, Wyrm crawled. He was in the shape of a serpent, so damnably huge that he could pass once around the earth and then bite his own tail ahead of him. He lived in caverns underneath the earth's crust; but he could, when he wished, crawl through rock as if it had been loose dirt. He lived in darkness, in dampness, in the cold. He stank fearfully, because his outer skin was always rotting, a runny putrefaction which made him itch, and which he tore away from himself by scraping his back against the granite teeth of the deep. He was lonely. He was powerful, because evil is powerful. He was angry. And he hated, with an intense and abiding hatred, the God who had locked him within the earth. And what put the edge upon his hatred, what made it an everlasting acid inside

[23]

of him, was the knowledge that God had given the key to his prison in this bottomless pit to a pack of chittering *animals*!

Oh, it was a wonder that Chauntecleer the Rooster, that a flock of broody Hens, a Dog, a Weasel, and tens of thousands of suchlike animals—and even that Ebenezer Rat—should be the Keepers of Wyrm! The little against the large. The foolish set to protect all the universe against the wise!

"Sum Wyrm," he roared all the day long, *"sub terra!"*

Yet so deaf were the animals to the way of things that even this dreadful announcement they did not hear. Chauntecleer went about crowing his canonical crows and planning his plans and blustering his Hens through another day, deaf to the cry and ignorant of his own purpose upon the earth.

Dumb feathers made watchers over Wyrm in chains! It was a wonder. But that's the way it was, because God had chosen it to be that way. A Rooster stood in the middle—and on one particular day, he was irritated by the fact that he couldn't finish his sunbath. But that's the way that it was.

[Five] *Wyrm acts—Cockatrice is born*

ast of Chauntecleer's land, upriver from him a good many miles, and near the mountains out of which the river flowed, was another land ruled by another Rooster. No communication existed between the two lands, because a forest stood between, and nations lay isolated in those days; so neither Rooster knew of the other, and what went on in either place went on unto itself.

Senex was this Rooster's name: Senex with his Back to the Mountains. In his Coop there were nearly a hundred Hens, because his rule had been a long one. He was very old; it was evident to everyone that he would soon die. His head was pink, bald around his comb; his toes, which had once been a source of pride to him, were thick and bent into four directions so that he walked with a peculiar shuffle and could not perch well on a roost. His eyes were failing. His crow had diminished to a henny kind of cluck, and he apologized a great deal—which infuriated him, but he couldn't seem to help it.

Two other problems he had: He would crow the morning in the middle of the night. His clock was off, and that sent his animals into a scurvy confusion. The hundred Hens would flock outside, prepared to work, and find that only the moon was there to shine on them. Back inside they would flock again, mumbling, clucking, shoving, and bitching a nasty bitch.

"Senex, button it," the bolder ones would grump. Young wives to old husbands take astonishing liberties. "If you can't crow right, Codger, don't crow at all, is what I always say. I say, button it, and give a Hen her sleep. Or sleep in the trees yourself. Which is to say, if saying can be heard by your bung ears, get out!"

"Sorry, sorry, sorry," the poor Rooster would apologize, and then despise himself for having done so—because he was Lord, after all.

In a moment every Hen would be asleep again; but Senex, the Rooster with his Back to the Mountains, would remain awake, miserably worrying about his other problem. Which was that he had no sons, no heir to assume his rule—either now, should he abdicate (and it crept upon him with painful frequency that he was, perhaps, already unfit to rule), or later when he died. He had produced no prince. A hundred Hens and—nothing.

Then, in the middle of the night, Senex would quietly weep.

He wept for his land. If he left no ruler behind him, the various powers in the land would break their backs against one another trying to seize rule, and the land would itself suffer. Peace would die when he did.

He wept for himself. For all of his past years of an ordained and gentle ruling, he received very little honor now. He was still carried in procession among his animals, and they still blessed him as he passed by. But that soon felt to him like a mock when his Hens forgot how to say "sir," and called him, instead, by his first name, and sometimes even forgot that. They fed him gruel and gossiped womanish things in his very presence, as if the whole Coop were their kitchen and he a baby in a bib. He had gotten no son on them.

And he wept for his name. Whatever they thought of *him*, at least the name of his father should be honored. But not only was it not honored, it would not even continue after him, because there was no son!

Thinking all these things, Senex would begin to curse and swear under his breath, angry with an old and useless anger, until he had cursed his tears away. And then he would go to sleep.

But because he was very old, he didn't even then sleep well. He dreamed.

"You fool!" his dreams would say to him—and even asleep he had the sense of a ghastly odor about him. "They ride you, Senex. They ride you mercilessly in your old age. They take advantage of every good thing ever you did for them. And they wait for you to die."

It was a half dream. The old Rooster was aware that he was asleep, aware of the Coop around him; yet his body was a lump of lead and he could move nothing. There was no vision to the dream, that he might see—only a mild and manicured voice, only the vile smell.

"It is the way of things," the aged Rooster answered in his dream. "I think it's time for me to die."

"Senex, Senex," the dream admonished him. "Die, perhaps. But die dishonored? Die weak? Die with your name befouled by a hundred ruinous Hens? Senex!"

"Sorry, sorry, sorry," said the Rooster.

"My dear Senex!" How the dream drooled his name. "Apologies belong to Hens and Rodents. But you are the Lord! Why, there's not a soul under heaven to whom you need apologize."

"I'm sorry," said the Rooster to his dream. And then, for apologizing, he apologized again: "Sorry." After that he hated his mouth mortally, because it wouldn't keep still. And he felt brokenhearted.

"Let it be," said the dream kindly. "I understand your dilemma. You feel a loss of power far before power should be lost to you. You are much misunderstood. And yet you feel constrained to reign over a thankless land. Am I right?"

Senex was comforted. "Yes," he said, panting and answering as fast as an old Rooster could, before the dream would fade. It was a good dream!

"And you have no son. A son would make your death honorable. An heir would preserve your name. A prince

[27]

upon any one of them would snap your Hens into order. Am I right?"

"Yes! Yes!" cried the poor old Rooster, almost giddy with the thought of it.

"Then I promise you that you shall have a son."

Suddenly the dream was over, and it was the morning. Senex jerked his head up and blinked into the grey light, surprised that that was all there was around him and suddenly feeling very lonely.

He was unusually silent all that following day, something which his Hens barely noticed, what with all their own personal primping and activity. He was trying desperately to preserve the good mood which the dream had given him, again and again remembering the words of it, and particularly its last promise to him: "And I shall have a son," he thought. Oh, he didn't do anything about *getting* a son. He was too old for that. But to remember the promise, he fought against heaven and earth and against the ease with which the elderly forget. Senex had a new thing in his soul. It was called *hope*.

On the following night the smell and the dream returned. It lasted all night long. Not everything could he remember from it; but some things clung to him:

"I promise you more than a son. I promise you your own life back again. Senex, Senex, if only you knew!"

"I'm young!" Senex cried in his sleep. "I can learn. Teach me!"

"Oh, bless you, proper bird!" the dream sang mildly. "Then learn this: You don't have to die. You can be born again, feather fresh and new. You can keep your land, but rule with a young vigor and with iron. And then you need not be remembered, Senex: But you will be seen and known."

This time when the dream passed, Senex walked straight over to the Hen who called him Codger and bit her viciously on the back of her neck. She woke with a

[28]

shriek, and the old Lord went away, immensely pleased with himself. There was a new strut in his step that day.

"I will tell you the secret of the ages," said his dream sometime later—during the day, now; for Senex had taken to sleeping all the time. To be awake had become disagreeable for him; to be asleep was very pleasant. He had begun to feed upon his dream.

"The secret of the ages," the stunned Rooster mumbled in return.

"I will tell you what God has hidden from everyone. God meant to keep it unto himself; but I know it and will tell it to you."

God has kept something back from me! The Lord of the land! thought Senex. He uses it only for himself? Well, then, it must be wonderful indeed.

"Indeed!" whispered the insinuating dream. "The wonder is this, that *you can be born again as your own son.* Thus the land remains yours, and the ruler is you. But you are young and healthy in your rule, and by a single crow you may kill a hundred Hens."

The old Rooster fell from his perch and doubled up in silent laughter, so that the Hens thought he was having a convulsion.

"Let it be!" he cried in a brittle voice, and the Hens were frightened. But he had cried, "Let it be," and so it was.

"Void the Coop!" roared his dream, a sudden, imperious commandment. "Hen for Hen, get them out of here! Lock the doors against them. No one but yourself! You and I shall be alone. NOW!"

Suddenly the Rooster felt his soul wither, and he was terrified. If he could have spoken, he would have apologized. If he could have run, he would have done so. If he had been able, he would have died; for the voice was not like the voice he had known. But he could do none of these things, being asleep. And he did as he was told.

[29]

With his eyes closed—asleep—he charged his Hens savagely, ripping feathers and causing the blood to flow, until every last Hen had scuttled screaming from the Coop. He did as he was told. The doors and the windows were locked, and he was alone with his dream.

The days passed, and the Coop became very hot inside. The Rooster ate much and grew fat, and the fat made his body all the hotter. And then, when the heat came to a certain temperature, Senex felt a wild pain in his loins, and his body did a strange thing. First it clucked, exactly as if he were a Hen. Then it squatted just above the ground, as strange desires drove him in spite of himself. Then it laid a small, leathery egg.

Senex, the Rooster with his Back to the Mountains, awoke.

The terror had left him. There was a fierce light in his eyes, now, because he had been given proof of the dream's promise, and he believed it with all of his being. An egg, after all, is an egg! And this Rooster worshiped his strange little egg.

He threw open the doors to the Coop and cried out in a voice so loud and majestic that everyone heard: "Here! Come and see, every one of you!"

They came. Something had happened to their Lord during his isolation; his voice was hard, wooden, and not to be denied. They came, and he showed them his egg.

"This shall be my son," he said, and the animals were amazed. "When he has hatched he will bear my name, and he will rule over you—righteous, just, and . . . punishing!" Oh, the old evils would be scoured clean!

The animals didn't know what to say. They didn't understand the light in Senex's eye. So they filed past the egg in silence and out again. But this time Senex commanded one Toad to stay in the Coop with him. And again the doors were locked.

The Toad was forced to sit upon the little egg, while

Senex fed him sumptuously upon bread and filled his head with all manner of wild sayings. The poor Toad held his peace and passed his time in fear.

When it became clear that the egg was about to hatch, the old Rooster called all of the animals into the Coop again. He hopped about on his crooked toes and chuckled to himself and shook his head violently at the joke which was about to be played. But the animals were there because they must witness this birth, and—he told them gleefully—they must welcome their new ruler.

"Apologize to you?" he cried again and again. "Apologize to a pack of ungrateful parasites? Ha! Don't look for it! Look for recompense!"

But, as no one understood his rambling, no one answered. They shrank from him, and they watched the egg.

It hatched. Better, it ripped apart. A new Rooster was born.

For seven days, as the animals began to come and go through the Coop, Senex sat and stared at his son with a wild intensity—saying nothing, but grinning and nodding with hungry satisfaction.

Then, on the seventh day, the Rooster chick began to grow a tail. The tail had no feathers on it and no hair. It was a serpent's tail. But it grew with an astonishing speed, and old Senex lost his grin. Very slowly a sense of cheat began to eat at his heart; and then he began to shoot glances at the other animals, who always filled the Coop to see this wonder.

The Rooster chick continued to grow, though it ate nothing at all. It was fed and nourished by the earth itself. As it grew, it developed grey scales underneath its body, from the throat to the tail; and the tail itself was covered all over with scales. Yet it had a rooster head and the wings of a rooster. But they were like fire, and its eye was red.

Senex, the Rooster with his back to the Mountains, began to feel the urge to apologize again, and he kept his

[31]

head bent very low—not only to hide from the gaze of his animals, but also because this thing of his ancient loins, this Rooster chick, had begun to glare back at him, coiling and uncoiling its tail.

On the fiftieth day since the arrival of the Rooster chick two things happened:

Senex could stand it no longer. The cold stare had broken him. He went to the door of his Coop, shivering, shaking his bald head, and chattering in a voice very weak: "Sorry, sorry, sorry, sorry, sorry."

The animals gathered and watched him, some of them with disgust, some with curiosity, and some full of pity.

One Hen saw her opportunity. She began a speech: "The wheel turns, Senex! And now we know the stuff the Lord is made of. Peck a Hen and pay for your trouble, is what I always say." She began to walk forward from the crowd. "Peck me and pay me, Codger! Now it's my turn—"

The Hen never finished her speech. She had a loud, husky voice; but another voice cried out now which swallowed hers entirely:

"Damn the name Senex!" screamed the monster from within the Coop. The animals froze, horrified. Senex snapped up his head without turning around. A look of infinite knowledge passed over his face, and despair.

"I am my own," the shriek continued, "and my name is *Cockatrice*!"

Then this was the second thing which happened. While every animal watched unmoving, Cockatrice stepped out behind the old Rooster, whispered something into his ear, and killed him—piercing his head through and through with its beak. Senex fell feather and bone into a little heap. Then Cockatrice swept the poor, exhausted body aside with its tail and began to rule in his place.

[six] Chauntecleer deals with Ebenezer Rat

obody had to tell thirty Hens where to sleep that night. Not one of them was going back into the Coop, once Nezer's name had been named and his guilt proven. But somebody might have told Chauntecleer where to crow compline, for the close of the day. He usually did that from the top beam of the Coop. However, the top beam of the Coop was now a long bunch of Chickens from one end to the other, sitting ghostly, patient and pillow still. No crowing there, unless one wanted to knock a Chicken off.

So Chauntecleer grumbled his way to a stump and crowed the close of the day from that. Then he went to see how Mundo Cani Dog was doing.

Mundo Cani had put his nose to use.

Immediately after crowing the crow of grief that morning, Chauntecleer had strutted round the Coop until he had found a hole through the wall. He was bitter with himself that he had never noticed it before; but now he could be certain that it was Nezer's own door into Chauntecleer's Coop because enormous Rat droppings were discovered immediately inside. And he marveled at the size of the Rat's entrance: Nezer had done himself proud.

Having found the door, Chauntecleer wanted to do something about it. He wanted Nezer to stay under the Coop until nighttime, so he wondered what might be large enough to plug the tunnel.

At that precise moment a storm of sniffles, followed by a rushing, mighty wind, sailed around the Coop. Mundo

Cani had just blown his—nose. And for the rest of the day the Dog lay belly flat upon the ground, his knees poking high above his back, his nose stuffed into the Rat's doorway. Chauntecleer took a particular pleasure in that arrangement.

"Me, mutt. It's me," he whispered now, because the night was mortally dark. "Have you heard anything?"

The Dog said something. But if his nose was under the Coop, so was his mouth; and who can understand a voice from underneath a chicken coop? After he said his something, Mundo Cani coughed; and his eyes rolled around like twin moons in his head, beseeching the Rooster with tears. Chauntecleer was tickled.

"Or have you *felt* anything?" he whispered.

What the Dog had next to say he said very fast, crossing his eyes. And then he coughed again, and his wide eyes nearly popped out. Chauntecleer was delighted.

"Surely," he whispered, "you haven't *smelled* anything?"

Mundo Cani said one word. It was a very short word and, by the sound of it, a sad word. But then he didn't have the time to say a second word, because his eyes filled up with water; his ears flew up from his head; and he sneezed.

All of the Chickens did a little dance on top of the Coop, and the Dog was blasted out of the hole, backward.

"You pump! You paragraph!" Chauntecleer hissed. "What are we going to do with noises like that? What *won't* Nezer know after such a speech?"

Mundo Cani hung his head and let a river run onto the ground. "This nose smelled one or two bad smells," he said, "but that is as it should be. It deserves punishment now and again—may it stick under your Coop forever for sneezing."

"All right, all right. Is the Rat still there?" Chauntecleer wanted to know. He was in cold earnest now, and the games were over.

[34]

"Pump is maybe better than Lummox. But Paragraph—this poor head does not know what such a name might mean. Yet if the Doctor—"

"The Rat!" Chauntecleer hissed directly into Mundo Cani's ear. "The Rat! Is Nezer still under the Coop?"

"There was no sound all the day long. Nor any noise at all," the Dog said. "This nose felt nothing move. It could feel anything—nits, tics, grubs—were they to move even a little bit; but it felt nothing move under your Coop, Doctor. So then it did a poor job?" The question was a mournful one. "Maybe since the *morning* he isn't there."

"If you haven't heard anything, then Nezer's there. It's the silence," Chauntecleer said quietly, "that announces him. One last egg was eaten before noontime. Ebenezer Rat is in there, Mundo Cani Dog." Chauntecleer was quiet for a moment. Then he said: "Watch, now; and wait." And he left.

It was Nezer Rat's eternal silence and his dark secrecy which made any plan to feather him so difficult. Who had ever seen Nezer, except as he was leaving? Who had ever heard Nezer? Why, the long Rat could slide past thirty sleeping Hens and a dreaming Rooster, and no one would ever know that he had been among them—except that Beryl or Jacinth or Chalcedony would wake in the morning with one less egg beneath her.

It was Nezer's deep privacy which Chauntecleer had to overcome with his plan. Somehow he had to get Nezer out from under the floor and up into the Coop; there the Rat would be on the Rooster's ground, and the Rooster might be able to do something then. Chauntecleer decided against luring the Rat out, decided for driving him out. But who would go under the Coop? Who could hurt a Rat? No, the question might better be: Who could *sting* a Rat?—for therein lay an answer.

The Rooster went a little distance from the Coop and stopped before a small mound of soft dirt. There was a perfectly round hole in the perfect middle of this mound. Chauntecleer set his eye to this hole and looked in.

"Tick-tock!" he whispered.

"Not now!" said someone down in the hole.

"Tick-tock, rouse it and come up here," the Rooster said.

"I'm busy sleeping." The voice hardly sounded like a voice. It sounded like tiny twigs snapping. "My children are all busy sleeping, and the door is closed. Good night. Hush and good night!"

"Sleep in the morning, Tick-tock; but get up here now. This is urgent."

"Mornings, you enormity, are for working. Nights are for sleeping, and you crew the nighttime in some little while ago. Therefore we are fast asleep. Punctual! Let urgent happen when it's scheduled. Good night." Tiny twigs snapping were beginning to sound more like large branches cracking.

"I crew the nighttime in?" Chauntecleer knew very well that he had.

"You are an excellent clock, friend Chauntecleer. Good night!" Crack! "Good night!" *Crack!*

Chauntecleer lifted his eye from the hole and spoke to himself: "I crew the nighttime in. Well, then, I will crow the morning in."

He bent over again so that his tail feathers looped high over his back. He stuck his jet-black beak straight down into the perfectly round hole of Tick-tock the Black Ant. And then he crowed a minor morning crow. Nobody heard it, except for a few hundred Black Ants, who began immediately to march out of the hole in three perfect lines. In the middle of the night, the Black Ants went to work.

Tick-tock stood atop his hole, crossing his arms, shaking his head helplessly, and watching his laborers labor at a damn-fool hour.

[36]

"Good morning and what is it?" he snapped to the Rooster. "Urgent had better be urgent."

"Believe it," Chauntecleer said. "I wouldn't be here unless it was."

Chauntecleer the Rooster was growing weary of irritations. It crossed his mind for the second time in a day that it would be good to have just one person for simple friendship and for talk. In this single, chilly moment—as he got ready to give instructions to a busy-brittle and punctual Ant—the Rooster felt lonely.

It started to rain. Not a heavy rain. Not a storm. Just a miserable drizzle which pattered all over the roof of the Coop and which blew a cold mist through the windows.

Chauntecleer crouched in a dark corner, waiting, and was heartsick.

"Ebenezer Rat," he cursed quietly to himself. All thirty of his Hens were getting wet on the top beam of the Coop. But they would not, nor could they, come into the Coop for shelter. They had to wait in their chilly place, and Chauntecleer had to wait in his; and the difference was that he was alone.

He held two strong, long, white feathers in his left claw. He could barely see them through the heavy darkness; but he felt them several times over and knew them to be exactly what he wanted: They were sharp and barbed, bright and steely in their strength.

Left and right Chauntecleer tipped his head for a sound; but if there was one below, the sounds above covered it up. Black Ants are mighty quiet. He didn't expect to hear Tick-tock or his reserves. And Nezer was smooth silence itself: He surely didn't expect to hear the Rat creeping through his gloomy depths. But when the two came together, then there should be some sound for the warning. That was what Chauntecleer listened for.

Yet silence and the rain continued. Once the Hens

clucked against the itchy rain and shuffled for a better perch above him; but then the hush settled down again.

Suddenly beneath the floor there was a scurrying. No voice. Not even a small cry. But the scurrying was desperate, like wind in a bottle, like someone holding his breath—a dry scratching sound which shot under the floor from one end of the Coop to the other. A body bumped the wall. Chauntecleer was inclined to jump, but he waited, shivering. The sound moved in a circle for a moment, then straightened out and aimed for Nezer's door through the wall.

A short, astonished bark came from that place. Then a truly painful yelping rang out. The Coop began to shake. Mundo Cani was caught, hurt, and trying to break free all at once.

"Oh, Ebenezer! Oh, Rat!" the Rooster swore, but he waited. He fought an urge, and he waited.

In that moment his battle instincts were annoyed: Nezer had created an excellent cover for himself in Mundo Cani's yelping. Chauntecleer lost all sense of the sound underneath the floor, and that gave the advantage to the Rat. How could Chauntecleer know, in this oily blackness, when Nezer was passing through his hole in the floorboards? How would he know the moment for attack?

Chauntecleer pulled a feather from his breast. He would lay it over the hole and then, perhaps, see its shadow white move at the Rat's entrance. With the feather in his beak he touched along the floor toward the hole, the beak brushing wood. Suddenly he knew precisely where the hole was. He didn't see it. He hadn't felt it. But immediately beside his ear he *heard* it: The Rat's breathing nose was there. Then a whole Rat and a silent mouth.

Ebenezer flew at Chauntecleer's throat and tore feathers away.

The Rooster went up on his claws, beating his wings together in front of him. Shock turned into ferocity. The Rat hunched, ready again for a spring. Chauntecleer's feathers shook out and stood away from his body, so that he seemed an enormous shadow. He hopped, head high, and hissed a taut threat to the Rat.

But night was Ebenezer's element. He slipped through the air like a lizard and seized the Rooster at the back of his neck.

So violent a convulsion shook the Rooster's body that the Rat fell away, and immediately Chauntecleer turned and leaped—beak, beating wings, and claws all forward at the Rat. The right claw came down on Ebenezer's back like a beam and clutched, gripped. But the Rat twisted himself rubberwise and buried his snout in Chauntecleer's stomach. There he began to gnaw. The Rooster did not let go. And while Nezer jerked and chewed at his flesh, he took one of the white arrow feathers into his beak and dug down at the Rat.

Mundo Cani had fallen quiet, though nobody knew just when he had. None but the rain made a noise. Silently a Rooster and a Rat were fighting. The Rat would kill if he could; the Rooster wanted only to finish the plan which he had.

Chauntecleer pulled his head away from the Rat's shoulder. His beak was empty and the feather gone. Ebenezer was an eating worm within his stomach; yet faithfully the Rooster held him. He took the second white feather into his beak, found a place in Ebenezer's other shoulder, and pushed. With sudden, almighty thrusts he pushed the barb of the feather deep into the Rat's hide.

It is a horror to fight an enemy altogether silent, whose one cry is the rip of his teeth through skin. Chauntecleer—beak empty for the second time—shattered the silence with a wild crow of victory, spun the Rat through the air behind him, and heard his body thump against the wall.

Then the fighters lay down. But it was Ebenezer Rat who had lost.

Forty-eight Black Ants, who had been biting the Rat's

tail, duly hopped off, formed a perfect line, and marched out of the Coop. But the two magnificent feathers which were hooked into Ebenezer's black hide would stay there until his own last day.

"Now, Ebenezer! Now, Rat, find you a hole," breathed the hoarse Chauntecleer from where he lay. "Find a hole, black Rat, which will let you pass through it like a secret. It will have to be a cave. And learn all over again how to sneak, now that you have two wonderful feathers to tell all the world of your coming. The Chicken eater chickened! Ha!" Chauntecleer barked. "Go with God, Ebenezer Rat; and forever leave my eggs alone."

Thirty shivering Hens plopped down from the top beam of the Coop and slipped inside, trusting without a doubt the crow they had heard. They tiptoed around the Rat, for they could see him now, and lined up on their roosts. Someone might have said something about what had taken place here; but as it happened, no one said a thing. They settled down close to one another and looked at one whom they had never seen before.

So this is Ebenezer Rat.

And while this gallery watched, Nezer got up and stumbled underneath his ungainly, lolling feathers. Stumbled away and out of the Coop by the door, since his holes were now impossible to him.

That was a nice sight, and everybody thought that it was time to dry out and to have a rest.

No, not everybody.

Someone was weeping hopelessly in the rain outside the Coop door. This was the kind of weeping which would soon become a wailing, and after that a howling. "Barood!" that someone wept, wailed, very nearly howled: "Barooooood!"

So Chauntecleer waited to do one more thing before he climbed to his perch, figuring that if he was to get some sleep, he had better say something now:

"If you come inside this Coop," he croaked, irritated for the last time that day, "you'll shut up. Understand, luggage? Some nights I can tolerate being awakened by your dreary trumpet. Some nights. Not tonight."

"Thags," wept Mundo Cani Dog as he stepped inside. "Thags," as he curled himself into a loop at the doorway. And then he, too, was quiet and there was only the rain. But a sensitive soul must know what an effort it was for him *not* to weep. His heart was woeful, for his great nose had swollen to twice its size.

[SEVEN] Something about the penalties of Lordship, together with Chauntecleer's prayer

At twelve noon on the following day, Chauntecleer the Rooster was to be found plotched upon a mud heap in the middle of a wet and runny field in the middle of a grey, rainy day. Spasmodically his wings slapped the mud around him and his head jerked with the bark of the little word "Ha!" His color was spoiled yellow in the rain, and everywhere his feathers stuck to his body.

It is a lesson, how one may pass quickly from the immortal feeling of triumph to the mortal mood of grumpiness. From midnight to noon Chauntecleer had made the transition: He was in a filthy mood. But then, he had a multitude of reasons, any one of them good enough to provoke the Dun Cow herself.

There was, first of all, the rain. The night had passed; the Rat had disappeared; but the rain had not. *Tap, tap, tap*—through the night and through the morning after it the chilly drizzle had persisted, and the boding clouds hung very near the earth. There was no sun, that sickly day, no cleanliness to crow to—only a leaden light which made breathing difficult, which sucked the green out of the leaves, and which made the muddy field feel like a hopeless hallway. Nothing whatever was solid in such a rain: The earth was slippery, water driveled everywhere, the sky merely dripped, and every standing thing lay down to weep. *Plot, plottery, plot, plot:* The rain fell into the puddles all around him, spinning out foolish circles. Nonsense! Ha and nonsense! Chauntecleer hated the drear rain, and he would have attacked a puddle if it would have done any good. But it wouldn't have—and so he was grumpy. His soul itself was damp.

"Ha!" he said, bitterly, blinking to keep the water out of his eyes and slapping the mud. "Ha! Cock-a-bullwhistle. Ha!"

Also, he had the throbbing pain of the wound in his stomach. In fact, the wound was the reason why he should be squatting in the mud at all.

When he had awakened that morning, he had heard the rain on the roof and had decided without a second thought that he'd stay inside, where dry was dry, even if it was also dim for seeing. He would crow lauds, the first crow of the day, from right where he was on his sleeping perch, and then go back to sleep. If that meant that the Hens' ears would ring on account of a nearby crow, and if that meant that Mundo Cani would feel rejected since his mat of a back had not been used for the crow, well, so be it. Chauntecleer had earned the right to crow from his perch.

But what no one had told him, and what he himself had absolutely forgotten, was that his wound had stiffened during the night and glued itself to his roost. The scab included the wood he was perched upon. So when he stood up to crow, he only gargled and tumbled from the perch. The scab had ripped open; the wound had begun to bleed afresh; the pain had shot backward all the way to his gizzard; and the Rooster was furious with himself for so foolish an action.

Then one other damnable thing happened, and he went outside into the rain, grumbling blackly to himself, and looking around for some sticky mud. Dripping mud would be useless. Thick, sticky mud was what he wanted. This he found in the middle of an open field. He pushed up a pile

[43]

of the stuff with his claws, kicking it out behind him and patting it smooth. Then he straddled the pile and settled down upon it as if it had been a nest of eggs to be hatched. It was his poultice.

"Mud, be nice to that cut," he said. "Mud, be a friend to me."

And then he sat all alone, with rivulets passing him by on every side, and looked at nothing.

"Hens!" he said. "God can cork, skewer, pluck, gut, and boil them, for all I care. Hens!"

For the Hens of his Coop had done that other damnable thing to send him *out* of his Coop. They were the ultimate, indisputable cause of his grumpiness. Neither the rain nor his wound could match them for botheration.

What the Hens had done was to try to comfort him. They had quick, feeling eyes for somebody's pain; and they had seen the blood run down his azure legs to the white toenails beneath. If their ears were ringing after that morning crow—that morning gargle, to be truthful—they didn't show it. Instead, all thirty of them gathered around the bleeding Rooster, clucking busy bouquets of sympathy and dipping their pretty white heads. They offered him water for his hurt, water for his forehead and his thirst. They peeped at his wound, shuddered, and kissed him fondly on his wattles. They draped their wings over him for the warmth, and they cuddled him.

Now, even that would have been all right. Chauntecleer could enjoy the cuddle of a pert and pretty Hen on a rainy day. In fact, that might be the quickest way to perk a Rooster up, ripen his comb to a violet red, and heal his wound. But—"Cock-a-HA-HA!" The pertest and the prettiest Hen, the plumpest and the proudest scoot of a Hen, was nothing more than a *Chicken* if she had to say "sir" in the middle of a cuddle!

"Lord God," Chauntecleer cried out from the middle of

a wide and soggy field, from the top of a mud pile, through the moist air, to the belly of the clouds grey from horizon to horizon: "I put it to you, who put me over this Coop. What good is a kiss if it comes with a 'Please you, sir'? That is a chilly kiss. And what kind of a love is it that curtsies? And where is companionship in fear?" Chauntecleer began to beat the mud on either side of him and to spit, as if there were bile in his mouth.

"I didn't ask for this," he shouted. "You, God—you bound me body and soul to it, and you never told me! Come down out of heaven and tell me why. I can be only one thing around these Hens: a leader, a commander, and ever right and never wrong. Do you suppose that I could put my head down and weep like that boat-headed Dog you sent me? Of course not! Oh, you know that very well. The Hens would panic and their world collaps̜e. Do you suppose that I could be afraid out loud? Even you don't suffer this loneliness—you who are never afraid. Do you suppose that I could make love to a 'Yes, sir'? Do you think that I could hold a 'Good of you, sir' close to myself and call it love? Of course not! Of course not! Oh, you know that almighty well indeed. I should line my roost with pots and pans and be as happy. Pots and pans can only clang—but all this sweet propriety of my mincing Hens is nothing more than the clang of a Chicken! Let the Lord God," Chauntecleer roared to the heavens, "let the Lord God himself come down and stand before me and give an accounting of himself—that he makes Roosters lonely! Ah, forget it," he grumped, suddenly tired of his prayer. "Go step on a mountain somewhere."

The Rooster slurped down deeper into his mud pile. His feathers were steaming gently, and his little eye cocked balefully at a slippery world.

"This, that, and the other," he mumbled to himself for

no reason at all. "This, that, and the other. This, that, and the other. Ha!"

Then he became aware of a little figure with him in the wide world.

"Blow it out your nose!" he said to a Mouse creeping through the field; but she only looked at him and didn't try to blow anything out of anywhere.

[eight] The Wee Widow Mouse makes herself known, as far as she is able, and after that Chauntecleer finds a treasure

Chauntecleer looked away from the Mouse and expected her to wander on to wherever she was going. She didn't. She stood still and looked at him.

Chauntecleer peered off at the iron-grey sky for a while. Then he poked around at the edges of his mud pile and slithered his backside around in order to make a better seat. When this was done, he glanced over at the Mouse, then quickly glanced away. She was still there, gazing at him, gazing directly into his eyes.

Chauntecleer whistled a tune out of the side of his beak. It was beginning to dawn on him that he was uncomfortable under this woman's gaze. In fact, it was downright embarrassing to be squatting on a heap of mud in the smack middle of a wide and empty field in the middle of the rain, and to have this small, watchful audience while he did.

Chauntecleer got up, turned a half circle so that his tail was aimed at the Mouse, and plotched himself down again. He counted up to one hundred fifty-seven.

She was gone, now. She went home. Good.

But he hadn't heard her go away.

But of course she was gone. Who would stand around in the rain for no other reason than to stare at a Rooster?

[47]

She had *crept* away, too polite to say anything to a royal bird, and that's why he hadn't heard her leave.

But it didn't feel as if she were gone away. In fact—

Chauntecleer snapped his head around so that he was looking straight over his back. She was still there, gazing at him.

"Did you hear what I said?" said the Rooster over his back.

The Mouse nodded. A drop of rain slipped off the end of her nose.

"Well?"

She didn't do anything. She looked at him.

"You know what it means?"

She shook her head.

"It means go home. Blow it out your nose: It means go home very, very fast. Move! Begone! I don't want you here!"

The Mouse kept standing where she was and looking at him.

"COCK-A-DOOD— Ack!" The Rooster started to crow, but the crow got stuck in his neck because his head was twisted all the way around. "So, then! Fine, then!" he said as he stood up. He made a great show of standing up. "Take this place, and I'll go find another. Perhaps you'd like a warm mud puddle."

Chauntecleer began to strut away, muttering. When he glanced back he saw that she was still looking at him, only she had bent her head sideways in order still to see him.

That did it! He ran at her, flapping his wings and spraying water out in two wonderful arcs. "BLOW IT OUT YOUR NOSE!" he shouted, and the Mouse began to cry.

Suddenly blow-it-out-your-nose sounded like a dismally stupid thing to say, especially since they were the only two creatures in all this wet field, and since rain makes creatures need one another. The Mouse was crying with wide-open eyes.

[48]

The Rooster sat down again upon his mud pile, this time facing her. And this time he waited for her to talk. But he didn't look her in the eyes, because she had never once taken her eyes off him, and he was ashamed.

Her tears flowed sadly through water already on her face.

When she was done crying, she said quietly, "My children," and then she stopped.

Chauntecleer didn't interrupt even her silence, now. He waited. She was so much soaked that at a distance she had seemed to him another piece of mud dropped on the field. She was remarkably thin, since her fur was pasted to her sides, and little, and tired—her bones so small they should have melted in all this rain.

"My children are in the river," she said.

"The river!" Chauntecleer breathed. "You came all the way from the river?" The river was several miles south.

She nodded. "My husband is dead," she said quietly.

"But your children—they are alive?"

She nodded, still looking at him. It was the same look which she had all along; but now for the first time Chauntecleer could see that it was asking many questions.

"But, Widow— You said they were in the river," Chauntecleer said, himself speaking quietly now. "The river moves very fast."

She nodded again. Perhaps she was nodding that he had her words correctly. Perhaps she was nodding that, yes, the river moved very fast.

"Widow," Chauntecleer said, "are your children all right?"

She shook her head.

"Are they in danger?"

She nodded, looking at him. "The river moves very fast," she whispered. Her voice made of the words a plain statement; but her eyes said: "*Why* should the river move so fast?"

[49]

"Then they need help?" Chauntecleer asked.

"They are on branches," she whispered so softly that he barely heard her. But she was looking at him as clearly as before. "We came downriver on branches. I tied them to branches."

"How did you get off, Widow? How did you come here? Can you swim? I need to know these things." Chauntecleer felt that he had to hurry up; he had to get as many answers as possible before her voice died away altogether.

"I couldn't untie them. God help me," she whispered, looking at him. "My husband is dead. He was killed under the Terebinth Oak."

"That is surely something to be sad about," Chauntecleer said; "and I, too, will be sad over the death of your husband. But, forgive me, Widow, not now. Your children are still alive. Tell me, where are the branches? What part of the river?"

"He wouldn't leave them alone. He wouldn't run. He fought them, and they killed him under the Terebinth Oak."

"Widow. Are the branches near the level bank?"

She gave him nothing. Neither a nod nor a no.

"Did the branches stop at the island?"

Nothing.

Chauntecleer blinked against his impatience. "There is a cove on this river. Did you pass a cove? Did your branches go into a cove? It's like a bite out of the side of the river."

Something picked at her memory. Her eyes came to focus. "The branches were caught by reaching arms," she whispered.

"Arms? Arms? Whose arms?"

"Crooked, broken. Cracking arms from above."

Impulsively, Chauntecleer stood up and walked, thinking. Of all the places along the river, the cove was the likeliest. The water ran too fast at the level bank. The island showed a vicious point against the current. Any-where—anywhere else the branches would have been shaken apart. But a whirlpool turned in that cove, drawing flotsam into it. It was a dangerous harbor. There were—Of course!

"Arms!" Chauntecleer cried. "Oh, Widow, why did you think they were arms? Those are the tree limbs that over-hang the cove! But, look: There's a whirlpool in that place."

"I wanted to feed them. They wanted to eat," whis-pered the Wee Widow Mouse. "There was no milk."

Chauntecleer spoke lowly, but urgently: "One more question. Do the branches touch the shore?"

The Mouse moved her mouth. Immediately Chaunte-cleer put his ear close to her mouth, but there wasn't a sound. And when he drew back to see her again, she was looking at him with clear, earnest, pleading eyes. Her eyes said, "Answer me."

"Dear Widow," he said, "I want to love your children. I want to see them living that I may love them. Can some-one step from the shore to these branches, or does some-one have to swim?"

Again her mouth moved without a sound. Her voice had finally gone away, but her lips were still making the words. Chauntecleer could see what they said. They were not answering his question. They said: "Why should the river move so fast?"

The Hens had been making the best of a rainy day. They scratched, fed, cleaned the Coop, and gossiped—all in-side the Coop. The scratching was useless, unless it was for the exercise, because a wooden floor and a little scat-tering of straw yielded neither grubs nor seed. The cracked corn on which they fed was not a joy, for it was too moist for their taste. Cleaning was plain business. Yet this is all that the weather had left for them to do—this, and gossip. But that gossip more than made up for a grey, thankless day.

They described Ebenezer Rat and his two careening wings a thousand times over—clucking, chuckling, and laughing outright, until it seemed as if the sun were shining in this Coop. They shook their thirty heads over the wounds which their Lord had sustained in the fight. Chauntecleer knew very well of the one wound in his stomach. But he had taken no notice of the fact that his neck, front and back, had been stripped of its feathers. This the Hens had seen immediately. They also could see where Chauntecleer had found two feathers long and strong enough to be planted in the Rat's shoulders: They were primary feathers, one from each of his wings. Without them the Rooster's flight would be a grievous desperation. There was much to talk about, much to cluck and mutter over, much grist for a good gossip on a rainy day.

Mundo Cani Dog just lay before the door all the morning long with his two paws on top of his nose. He was trying to cover it up, but that was impossible. A spying Weasel might cheerfully have thought that the Dog was dead, except that once in a while he would sigh so powerfully that he blew up a cloud of dust from in front of his nostrils, and the dust made the Hens to cackle and bitch.

Suddenly the Dog raised his head. Nobody had heard anything, but he had heard something: His hearing was remarkable. But a moment passed, and he put his head back down again with a sigh. With a thump, too, which caused thirty Hens to hop.

Then he heard it again: "Mundo Cani! Dog, get out here! I need you!" That was clear enough, even if it was still far away. Chauntecleer had a crowing voice.

"Beryl, you too! I want you both!"

The gossiping stopped, and all the Hens went still. The Dog ambled out, and the Chicken fluttered behind.

"Oh, Doctor," the Dog murmured when he saw Chauntecleer squadging through the mud at a distance. "Such a stinking world that we live in to do such a thing to you. I am maybe ill luck and maybe should go away." For even at that distance the Rooster looked like a boiled soup-bone.

His chest, his stomach, his wing pits, and the loins between his legs were covered with a foul crust of grey mud, which had dried, hardened, and cracked. It was an odd casing to be walking in; but he was walking in it. But who can walk with a spade between his legs? He waddled. He rocked left and right.

His neck was skinny, pink, and featherless. It was a bent finger coming out of his shoulders, a sadness to see on one so royal.

And on his back was—what? A mud lump? A dead fish? Why, if the Rooster would only stand up straight, it would fall off and he would be rid of it. But he waddled crouched over, as if he wanted the morsel to *stay* on his back; and that, of course, made waddling an even greater difficulty.

"Dog, you are a wizard!" the Rooster crowed. Never mind the way he looked; Chauntecleer crowed like healthy thunder. "And Chicken, you surely know what you're doing. Don't ever let anybody tell you that your brains are maple wood. When somebody says that he needs you," crowed Chauntecleer as he puffed along, "you know that he doesn't mean it. Prophets! Providential geniuses! You know he only wants you to gape at him until he dies."

"Oh, no, Doctor," said the Dog whose nose was a log. "That's not what you meant. Forgive my speaking up, but it seemed to me that you needed us."

"WELL, THEN SHAG IT, YOU SUITCASE! GET OVER HERE!"

Mundo Cani Dog could run very fast when he had to. And Beryl came flipping behind.

"That's good to see," said Chauntecleer when they were near. "I need your speed, Mutt. Beryl," he said, "hold still and be tender."

The Rooster laid the Mouse, who had been borne upon

[53]

his back, on Beryl's clean back. The Wee Widow Mouse was asleep, and so she was no help to the one who carried her. "You will take this one back to the Coop. Warm her. Feed her. Bring her back to life. And for the Lord's sake, be quiet around her while she sleeps. Beryl," he said, "walk tenderly."

"I will, my Lord," said the Hen. Chauntecleer watched her narrowly to see whether her walk was indeed a tender one. It was.

"Dog, squat down," he commanded, and Mundo Cani went down in the mud. Chauntecleer climbed onto his back and grabbed the mangy fur in either claw.

"Do you know where the river is?"

"In my childhood," sighed the Dog, "I played at the edge of the water. My reflection I saw, once, when I was old enough to know evil. My nose—"

"You know where the river is. Run, Dog! Skin the wind! Run to the cove which is west of Liver-brook. MOVE!"

And a Dog did skin the wind. Mundo Cani had a talent which nobody would have suspected: He could run like any horse at a full gallop. He spun clots of mud out from under his paws with every wide, wild stride. The muscles in his hips and withers rolled, snapped, and tightened with perfect power; and the wind in Chauntecleer's face blinded him.

The Rooster was hard pressed to hang on. But he did. He stuck out his wings for the balance, leaned forward, crowed for pure joy at the speed underneath him, and gripped the sparse fur with all of his strength. Mundo Cani had a talent indeed!

The miles were minutes, the green hills a gone-again blur, the trees a constant danger avoided, the rain tiny bullets in Chauntecleer's face.

They sped up a long rise and fairly flew over the top of it. There Chauntecleer saw a valley; and in the bottom of it, the grey river. So many miles, so quickly!

[54]

Now down the side of the valley, with barely a paw on the ground.

The river had looked flat and still from above, a grey weight at the bottom of a valley. But as they plunged down to it, Chauntecleer saw violence in the water. The current whirled and eddied near the shore; at the center of the river that current went flat out in one direction: westward toward the sea with tremendous might. The rains had swollen the river. But how, thought Chauntecleer, could loose branches and Mice survive on the face of that water? And why, for the Lord's sake, would they *want* to take such a trip?

A cluster of trees showed where the cove was to their right. Between them and the trees pumped the dark brown Liver-brook, thick with water. Mundo Cani never paused, but took the brook all in a single leap, touched land on the other side, and galloped. He ran with the river. Chauntecleer was surprised to find that so much water and so great a current, choked with so many logs, branches, and shunt, made not a sound at all.

Then Mundo Cani sailed into the cluster of trees.

Not the Dog, but the Rooster was breathing hard as they stared at the jam of wood spinning in the cove. Tree limbs from above *were* holding the flimsy island in place; but they wouldn't much longer, because the tree limbs and the island were untwisting one from the other. And then there would be no hope for it at all.

"She said that she tied them to the branches," Chauntecleer panted. "Can you see them? Can you see them? What do you see?"

"What are they?"

Chauntecleer had forgotten to give the Dog any reason for their trip. "Her children. The Mouse's children."

"Oh, Master of the Universe!" Mundo Cani began to weep on the spot.

[55]

"Not now!" the Rooster barked. "Look for them. What do you see?"

It was like trying to spy a friend on a merry-go-round. This mass of wood had many hidden parts to it, all of it going in circles. The more Chauntecleer stared, the more he didn't see what was really there. Wood was there. Branches, as the Mouse had said; twigs, stems, limbs, leaves, branches: broken and whole, naked and barked, rotten and dry and white above the water. But the Rooster began to see other things. Bones. Shattered ribs. Choppy, dry fingers clutching at the air. Pieces of crushed skull. A spinning cemetery of bones; and for just a moment it made him afraid.

"There!" shouted the Dog. His vision was remarkable. "What's that?"

Chauntecleer saw the branches again. "Where?"

"There." His nose turned circles, pointing.

"Mundo Cani Dog! There they are!"

It was a bird's nest crammed tightly into a dense part of the branches, a mere fist of twigs. The nest was not tied to the branches; but the children were tied into the nest. Many strands of hair had been patiently tied, crisscross, over the top of the nest; and Chauntecleer could see bulges in the webbing, bodies bumping it.

He leaped to a low branch on the tree beside him, found his balance, then leaped to a higher branch. This way he climbed the tree to the place where it leaned out over the water. Now he could walk along a limb, flipping his feathers to keep balance. The limb sank underneath his weight. His wings went out, but he didn't fall. By his beak and his claws he grappled his way down droopy branches, until he hung, head down, directly over the turning island.

Out of the corner of his eye he saw a part of the shore which he had not seen before. There was something white there, like a stone or a pillow, or salt. But in the middle of it was a burning patch of brilliant color. There was no

[56]

time for the looking. He dropped down.

With the sharp edge of his beak Chauntecleer ripped the hair from the nest. Seven tiny Mice squeezed down into the farthest corner, terrified. He stuck his wing into the nest; that didn't help matters any.

Chauntecleer struggled with his own impatience at tiny bits of stupidity. Simply, they did not know that they should climb this monstrous wedge to safety, and they would have to be told.

"Listen to me, children," Chauntecleer said. "Your mother is beautiful. She has a coat as warm as sleep. She has a dry place in which to sing to you. But do please listen to me: She isn't here. And the dry place isn't here."

Perhaps not his words themselves, perhaps his tone and the steady look in his eye, spoke to them. For they looked back at the Rooster, somewhat sadder but less afraid.

"So she sent me to you with this message. Come. Come closer to hear it."

One did wriggle closer. Chauntecleer's heart beat violently.

"She said, 'A Rooster will give his wing to you.' This wing. And I'm the Rooster. Forgive me: I have a bad voice, nothing like your mother's. But that is truly her message. And she said, 'You, my children, must hurry to climb onto his wing.' Do, please, children, climb onto my wing."

To Chauntecleer it seemed as if the river and the whole world were turning circles, while the thicket-island stood still. Once again, in the flash of passing, he saw white upon the shore. But then he shifted his weight; the island dipped; and not a Mouse was climbing!

"Listen. Listen to me." The Mice were watching him; it broke his heart how much their gaze resembled their mother's. "Listen. The most important part of her message is something that only the smartest of you can understand. The others are too foolish to understand it; but one of you is much smarter than the rest. She said, 'I am

[57]

waiting for you.' Now what do you suppose that means?"

Immediately one Mouse—his pink skin so thin that his bones could be seen within—climbed onto the wing by impossibly small claws. Two more followed.

"There's the smart one!" Chauntecleer hooted, restrained. "Oh, God bless the smart one. And there's a brave one, too—braver than all the rest, God willing. *He* will know that you have to climb all the way to my back—dangerous, dangerous climb!—and he will know that you have to burrow beneath my feathers."

So the Brave One squirmed past the Smart One, and a procession of naked children needled a Rooster's shoulder while he held himself almighty rigid. Dizzy, swallowing crow after urgent crow until he choked, counting the children before his hot eye, he held still until the last Mouse was snuggled in place—and then he exploded.

Across the nodding island, up with a wild leap, barely grabbing a branch in his claw. The island bowed and floated away. Chauntecleer's tree sank beneath his weight; the Rooster's tail touched water and was tugged by it. He said a curse word. When his other claw would not go high enough to find a grip because of the crusty mud between his legs, he said a dozen more curse words and damned the river pulling at him. There was no island, now. He hung all alone, like bait, in the middle of the cove, heavy with mud from his neck to his tail.

It was at that particular moment that his eye caught the white object on the shore. Perhaps in the desperation his senses were sharper, because he recognized it. Not salt; it was a Hen! But no Hen he had ever seen before. And the color on her was vermilion, blazing at her throat.

All at once Chauntecleer found some more energy inside of him for getting his other claw to the branch. It was wonderful how quickly that claw took hold, and how powerfully claw followed claw up the droopy branch. Into the tree he went like a whizz, across the limb, and down the trunk like a born squirrel.

[58]

"Mundo Cani, open your mouth," he roared.

Mundo Cani opened his mouth. He wanted to put a word into it, or perhaps a whole sentence. But before he could do that, Chauntecleer stuck his head in and pecked at the tongue until it went backward into the throat.

"Gug!" said Mundo Cani Dog. And Chauntecleer said, "I understand. I understand totally, good friend. Keep your tongue where it is. I've some passengers for you."

And hastily, but with marvelous care, he picked the Mice out of his back feathers one at a time and set them down in Mundo Cani's mouth.

"Not a very dry place," he said to them. "And it's a certain fact that that clog in the back isn't your mother. But it's the way to your mother, children. Your coach! And your mother will rejoice to see you again. Dog, shut it!" he said.

The Dog did, and his eyes began to water.

"If you sneeze, leatherhead," the Rooster roared, "I'll plug your nose and then it will blow up like a balloon!"

Mundo Cani shook his head. That wasn't why his eyes were watering.

Now Chauntecleer scrambled down the oily shore, to the place where he had seen the Hen.

She was lying unconscious on her back, her small claws balled on top of her. At her throat her feathers were crimson and beautiful. But her tail feathers were lapped in water, and she was wet to the roots. Her beak was open. But she was not dead. And she was so beautiful.

Now Chauntecleer the Ready did a most unready thing: He sat down and stared.

Perhaps if he had first seen her while she walked among a flock of Hens, clucking and pouting, this might not have happened to him. But he saw her in her weakness. He saw her lying open, where anyone in the world could have come by and hurt her. He saw her loose, sleeping, and without protection whatsoever. He saw her truthful, when she was not pretending to be anything else than a purely white Hen with fire at her throat. He saw her when she didn't see him back. He saw her lovely.

Chauntecleer stood up. Then he sat down again. Again he stood up; he ran to find Mundo Cani, but the Dog had gone; so the Rooster returned and sat down—close enough to touch her, should he work up the nerve. Well, the fact is, Chauntecleer the Rooster wanted to wake her up. But he didn't know how. He was embarrassed. Her sleep embarrassed him.

He tried a hoarse little crow. A cough, really. But the Hen remained still. If she didn't notice the rain, which fell everywhere upon her stomach and wings, how could she notice the clearing of one's throat?

So Chauntecleer apologized aloud several times, and then he crowed. He crowed a round, loud, morning crow—lauds, with the full flapping of his wings and the thrusting of his head. Then he watched her and saw her eyes roll underneath their lids. But that was all.

He was in an anguish.

"I can't carry you," he pleaded. "I can barely walk. You *have* to wake up!"

Then he reached out and touched her. He snapped back, afraid to be caught in the act. But it did no good.

After a long debate with himself, he took courage and shook her. Her head lolled back and forth. He shook her again, and this time she took a sharp breath and began to cough.

"Glory, glory, glory," Chauntecleer mumbled, but he got away from her and watched.

The Hen rolled over onto her stomach with the coughing and slowly stood up. She had to push at the ground in order to stand, because she was so weak; but she tottered and stood. Chauntecleer unconsciously patted his wings together. Her eyes took on a light. Around at the river she looked, around at the weather as if she didn't understand either one. Then she looked, suddenly, at

Chauntecleer himself. And the Hen screamed.

It was a scream of white terror.

Chauntecleer's stomach turned immediately to water and his legs trembled. "Don't," he said, still patting his poor wings together and hopping from leg to leg.

But the Hen only screamed the more—crazy, unaccountable screaming. Her mouth wide open, she turned and tried to run away. But it was a sadly broken run, with her wings slapping at the ground. She kept slipping toward the river.

Chauntecleer couldn't go after her; he felt too guilty. But he couldn't stand still and watch her pain and do nothing—especially because he *did* feel guilty. So he said, "Oh, please, don't," and hoped with all his heart that she would stop of her own accord.

She didn't. She came treacherously close to the current. Her screaming took on syllables and resolved into a single word, repeated again and again without meaning and without end. "Cockatrice!" she was screaming so full of terror: "Cockatrice! Cockatrice! Cockatrice!"

Chauntecleer could stand it no longer. Every instinct in him was appalled to see her so careless of her life. In spite of himself he began to run after her. Nor was his run any better than hers. He, too, stumbled on account of his mud cast; but he ran with a purpose.

He caught up with the Hen. With his beak he grabbed the back of her neck, and he wrapped his wings around her. She fought him wildly, flailing her wings and beating him on the sides of his head; but he didn't fight back. He just held her as tightly as he could. And together they began to slip into the river.

She turned her head. With a ghastly determination the Hen tried to pierce the Rooster's eyes with her beak. But Chauntecleer put down his head, letting her cut his neck, and he started to cry. Not for any pain he cried, but because he was exhausted; and because the weather had been so damnably careless; and because she was hitting him at all. He held her tightly, and he cried.

Then, as they churned in the water, Chauntecleer's cast of mud began to melt and to break up. Chunks of it floated off, or sank; and his wound opened again and began to bleed. His blood colored the water.

It was the blood which made the Hen gutter in her throat and finally stop her screaming: for in a moment she was staring at her own feathers, where it stained her. Then she searched the Rooster before her, gazed at his chest and stomach, where there was no longer the grey mud but golden feathers and a bleeding wound. She closed her mouth and looked stricken in her soul. "You're hurt," she said strangely. "You can be hurt. Oh, look how badly you are hurt."

Chauntecleer was able to pull her to shore, still holding her tight, tighter than ever. And the two of them lay down in the rain for a while. Both of them were trembling violently. Both of them were crying.

[NINE] *Through autumn Chauntecleer's*
Coop is a hospital, though one
full of good cheer

The rain never stopped.

Sometimes it was no more than a chill mist sitting on the air; other times it came down suddenly, like an angry fist, and the Coop shuddered against it. The sky stood iron above. And the weird wind was ever out of the east.

The trees lost their leaves, but there was no beauty in it this year, nor any color but rot. It was as if they had simply given up to the moisture and the cold, and forgotten life. Nor was there any crackling of dry leaves, nor the sharp scent—clean and musty—of falling leaves, nor the blue bite of the year going out. Damp foliage was stripped from the trees by an everlasting rain. The naked trees shivered. That was all.

But if mud and a bleak season lay all around, then Chauntecleer's Coop was a warm, blessed island in the middle of it all. This little company of creatures was proof against dreariness, and together they were very happy.

On account of the strange weather, they lived in an unending twilight; yet the Rooster must have had a rising and setting sun on the inside of him, for lauds and prime he always crowed on time; terce, sext, and none he observed ever on the button; vespers and compline he kept as they should be kept—and his small society was kept very well that way.

Chattering and motion and light and warmth filled the

[63]

Coop, as if it were a little furnace in a dark land. Food went into stomachs; gossip attended every ear; and the good cheer of the morning made waking a pleasant thing, while friendship—which filled the evenings—made sleep a good conclusion. The creatures were happy, because they were busy with good and important matters:

Four adults and seven children needed constant care, for they were convalescing. And thirty Hens, a Weasel occasionally visiting, a contingent of Black Ants, a Fox of Good Sense (Lord Russel by name), and several others were all more than willing to give these sick ones that care.

Four adults: Chauntecleer himself healed more quickly than anyone else. This was not just because he had so strong a constitution, one well able to knit even the most open wound. But this was also because his spirits were so high. Chauntecleer laughed enormously and often, these days. He talked much; and he would talk on any topic available, to anyone who asked a question. And, given more than two ears listening to his words with earnest attention, the Rooster began to fancy himself a philosopher. He stared at the ceiling and spoke grandly of God and of the ways of the Deity; he disclosed the hidden patterns of his effective rule; most particularly, he discoursed on beauty—female beauty—its attraction to the male—the special appeal of the color crimson—especially when crimson is placed, by nature, like a blossom at the throat of a Hen. And he smiled in his sleep these nights, Chauntecleer did, because his dreams were all good. And he worked trills and cadenzas into his crows. And he healed very quickly.

Ah, beauty! There was a thirty-first Hen in Chauntecleer's Coop—she of the burning, crimson throat. Her name was Pertelote (though Chauntecleer seldom reduced his naming her, or made it anything less than the full: the Beautiful Pertelote). She healed more slowly than he did because her illness went deeper, because this land was strange to her, and for another reason: The Beautiful Pertelote almost never spoke about herself. Not to Chauntecleer, who so often found cause to sit next to her; not to Beryl, who wanted so badly to help the Lady, but who didn't know what to do since the Lady wouldn't tell her of her hurt. To be sure, the Lady talked.

"My Lady slept poorly last night," Beryl would say privately to her. "I mark how she whimpered and wept in her sleep. And once she cried out. Dreams can be doused, Lady. Please, ma'am, let me give you a potion before tonight. Or tell me what your dreams are that I can make the proper mix."

But the Beautiful Pertelote would speak of things vastly different from what Beryl had in mind: "Beryl, have you always lived in this Coop?"

"Aye, ma'am." A brief pause for the Lady's wanderings. And then: "Is it your breathing? Does your breathing torture you?"

"Then you have always known the Rooster of this household?"

"That I have, ma'am."

"So golden his feathers, and redder than fine coral his comb. His nails whiter than the lily flower. Has he always borne his head so proudly?"

Beryl blinked. "That is his manner, ma'am."

"Ah."

"What will my Lady eat? Please you, ma'am, you must eat. If you'll tell me what likes you, I'll grind a little mustard seed into it, that you may mend. Or will you tell me where the pain lies inside of you?"

"Has he always been a Rooster?"

"Ma'am?"

"Has this Chauntecleer always been a Rooster? Was he ever anything else beside a Rooster? Was he ever but the *image* of a Rooster?"

"Forgive me, ma'am. Let me get you a drop of water."

[65]

"You don't understand what I ask you."

"My Lady excites herself. She breathes too fast, and that is her pain. Let me bring you a wee cup. I'll warm it with an herb or two."

"Beryl?"

"Ma'am?"

"You are very kind to me."

"Ma'am."

Beryl had come to love the Beautiful Pertelote immediately. But, finally, the poor Hen had simply to guess what ailed her Lady, and she had to mix her medicines without a true knowledge of the pain. She used nard mostly, for that seemed most to ease the Lady. But *seeming* is not *certainty*, and that distressed the anxious nurse. Pertelote would speak about herself to no one.

Not even to Chauntecleer. Chauntecleer had to learn what he could about her past and her arrival in his land from the third victim in this Coop-shaped hospital. And even the information which he gathered from the Wee Widow Mouse was next to nothing.

The Wee Widow Mouse and her seven children had a dry room all to themselves. They had moved into Ebenezer Rat's old nest beneath the floorboards. There they found food, furniture, and bedding enough to make them peaceful and to help them heal nearly as fast as Chauntecleer.

The Widow had had dreadful dreams too, at first. Some of the Hens had supposed these dreams to have come out of the air, from the evil fumosity which still murked through Nezer's tunnels. But the words which the Mouse said during her dreams had nothing to do with the Rat. Rather, they were spoken to a husband who was not there, and they described things which the Hens had never seen before. Soon the dreams passed, and the Mouse settled down to being a mother, apologizing many times a day for her seven children. The tiny Mice figured that every

Chicken's wing in the world was made for climbing into. Hens woke up with the Widow's children snuggled under their feathers.

Chauntecleer could get the Widow to talk about her children anytime. But every time he turned the conversation to her trip downriver, he saw all over again the staring little Mouse whom he first met in an open field.

"But why would you take that trip?" he would ask in the middle of another sentence. "What could make you do such a thing?"

Then the Mouse would grow silent. Her body would seem to shrink; and she would only look at him. She would step backward, as if there were a punishment coming to her from somewhere. And when he talked softly, assuring her again and again of his kind thoughts toward her, the look would only change, filling up with many questions as eyes fill up with tears.

All that Chauntecleer could patch together was that it had been a long, long, dangerous ride. The trip had started out in sudden panic. Nobody had planned on it; therefore nobody had planned *for* it (although, Chauntecleer thought, the Wee Widow must have acted wonderfully fast, because he remembered how skillfully the hair had been woven over the bird's nest). All of the women on the many branch-boats launched were strangers to one another. And when the branches were snatched by the current, some of the women were drowned straightaway, because they had no experience with water or with wood, and because one did not know how to help the other. Fear separated them. In the end there had been, besides the Hen, whom the Widow was now so grateful to know, two other women on the Widow's branches; but one had died of certain wounds during the night. The other might still be alive somewhere, but that was doubtful. She had gone raving mad one day, skittering all over the branches and chattering nonsense until she announced that she was going home; and she dived into the water. The Widow had not seen her again—not even to come up for air. She had been given a kind of hopeless courage by that drama, to think nothing, speak nothing, do nothing, all on account of her children. On the next day her branches were caught by the reaching arms.

This was, of course, not much for the Rooster to know. And it didn't come all at once. Over many days and with several tricks he learned this information from the Wee Widow. But every time he said, or even hinted, "Why? Why did you take the trip at all?" the Widow went deadly silent, totally ignorant of the importance of causes to rulers who make decisions. Instead, her eyes returned the "Why?" to *him*, and neither did he have an answer. So much the philosopher he was not; and his own ignorance before her eyes hurt him.

After their first meeting, the Wee Widow Mouse never again mentioned her husband or his death or the Terebinth Oak. That was the only picture which Chauntecleer had of anything *before* the trip, and he didn't understand it at all.

The fourth victim in the Coop hospital took the longest time of all to heal. Even Pertelote was breathing better—her cough gone, her breath able to handle a song now and again—before this one healed. This one moaned much in his pain. He moaned at the level of a shout. And he shouted his moans at any given ascension of the sun, but most especially at night.

When all the Coop had settled into sleep, this one would have his most stabbing pains: "Ignore it!" he would suddenly moan. "Put it out of your minds! Beryl, bring me no water! It is too much a burden for the least of you to consider what I am enduring; and I would not have the least of you suffer my suffering. Not a drop, Beryl! Not a moist handkerchief! But sleep, sleep on."

And should one or another of the sleepers happen acci-

[68]

dentally to awaken, this mourner would moan: "Wait! Be patient! Patience you gentle folk have in abundance. Wait—for I am going outside in a little. I'll carry this torment out to the weather. But you—you sleep with the peace which God has given to you."

Then he would duly step outside of the Coop; and there he would bellow his moan with the quietness of a cannon: "MAROOOOOONED!"

Mundo Cani's problem was that tiny Mice had bitten tiny pieces out of the roof of his cavernous mouth—not to mention a cramp in his tongue.

But, ah, beauty! None of this moaning ever awakened Chauntecleer from his good dreams, so joyful had the cock become. And let it be unwritten what grief such oblivious rejection caused a Dog.

[TEN] *The winter comes, with snow and with a marriage*

he raining never stopped. From horizon to horizon, the clouds were locked in place, and the earth was shut up. An east wind—an odd wind to command the weather—brought this wetness and never stopped bringing it.

But perhaps God looked down from his heaven and had pity upon the Coop, for a merciful change occurred in the rain. It became snow. And where water as rain was mere misery, the same water as snow was a soft delight: A hard freeze made the ground bony and firm; snow followed to whiten and to reveal the gentle contour of that ground; the cold air snapped life into the creatures who ventured forth to walk on it; the forest greeted them, tinkling and clinking as if its great trees had tiny voices—and more than any of that, the Coop became muffled in its warmth, because snow drifted up the outside of its walls.

Now the place was no longer strange to the Beautiful Pertelote, and she sang some clear, haunting melodies. Her singing was like the moon in a wintry night—sharp edges, hard silver, slow in its motion, and full of grace; so it took the place of so much that was missing in those days, for there was no moon. And in this season of the snow, one other fine thing happened. Chauntecleer and the Hen of the blazing throat were married.

Early one morning, before lauds and before any sleeper had awakened, Chauntecleer had crept to Pertelote's side in order to talk with her. He heard the wind outside; and he heard, from a great distance, the ice on the river shooting off its mighty guns, for the night was very cold.

"You are a singer," Chauntecleer said in a low voice. The Beautiful Pertelote moved in order to show that she was awake. She raised, then lowered, her head.

"Some of God's creatures sing. Some very few are singers. You, Lady, are among those very few."

Bang! went the river ice; and Chauntecleer was suddenly pleased to hear it, because it made him feel all the more snug with her who listened to him.

"Will you sing a melody for me now?"

She hummed for him a quiet melody like ringing crystal, neither clearing her throat nor raising her head first. It was as if the melody had always been on the rim of her soul, waiting for the touch to release it. And Chauntecleer was moved. This melody was for no one but him; it was offered at his request; it was so immediate, so ready, but altogether new. So he felt a little more bold to ask the thing which had long been on his mind.

"My Beautiful Pertelote," he said about the melody, when it was done, and he held his peace for the moment.

And then he said, "Don't be angry for my asking this; but listen and then answer me. It's not a hard question. It's an important one." He waited. "My Beautiful Pertelote, are you afraid of me?"

She raised her head and looked at him. "No," she said.

Chauntecleer waited, then blinked; and then *he* cleared his throat. He thought there would be more to her answer than that, since there had been so much to the question. "But there was a time," he began again, "when you *were* afraid of me, isn't that so?"

"No, never," she said easily.

"So, you say," he said lamely, searching for words, "never."

"Since I have lived in this Coop, Proud Chauntecleer," she said, and his heart leaped to hear her speak of her own accord, "I have looked at you with wonder. I have never been afraid of you."

Bang! went the river. "Does wonder," she said, "look

[71]

like fear to you? That would be foolish."

"Oh, no," he said. "I know wonder and I know the difference. But I don't know what to *do* with wonder when I see it in you. Wonder is also different from respect— greater than respect—because I know what to do with respect when I see it in the other Hens. I command it. And I draw away from it. But wonder . . . You are not like any other Hen to me."

The Beautiful Pertelote smiled and said nothing.

Bang! The ice exploded, grinding against itself. And Chauntecleer went back to his earlier question, because it truly bothered him.

"Forgive me: Was there *ever* a time when you were afraid of me? Even before you came to my Coop?"

He was trying to focus upon a particular time without actually naming that time. He was afraid that if he said, "When we first met on the shore of the river," he might resurrect dangerous feelings all over again, and then everything would be lost. Such a delicate game he played.

Pertelote said, "No, never."

Chauntecleer popped. "But you screamed at me!" There was his great anguish and the memory that knifed him. And immediately when he had said the thing aloud, he held his breath to see what she would do. Maybe, remembering, she would begin to scream again, and then what?

But she only said, "Yes, I screamed at you."

"Oh, Pertelote," he went on in spite of himself, "you ran away from me. And when I held you, you tried to blind me. Do you remember that?"

"Of course I do. Yes, I did those things to you."

"Then you were afraid of me."

"I'm sorry about it, Chauntecleer."

"But you *were* afraid of me!"

The ice cracked and rumbled; the rumbling came even through the earth. She waited until it was done, and there was pure, dark silence.

"No. I have never been afraid of you."

Now Chauntecleer heard more than the words. He heard the tone of her voice. More than that, she was talking straight to the frightful moment and still confessing her peace with him. Therefore Chauntecleer—who simply could not let it lie—took courage and probed further:

"If you weren't afraid," he said slowly, "what then?"

"Proud Chauntecleer," she said so softly, "you always think more thoughts than someone has said to you. I was afraid. But I was not afraid of you. I was—" Pertelote broke it off. This was the first time since she had come to Chauntecleer's Coop that she was talking about herself. It was difficult to do.

"I was afraid of what I saw in you," she said.

The Rooster's head came up erect and he knew a chill. "What you saw in me. You saw something in me to terrify you? What?"

There was a long silence. Then Pertelote spoke very carefully.

"Chauntecleer, what I thought I saw in you was not there. What I saw I should not have seen. My seeing was not true: The thing was not there, nor could it ever be there in you. I know that. My imagination made me afraid. But I was not afraid of you."

So kindly she tried to reassure him. But reassurance without a fact or two left the poor Rooster in a fit of his own imaginings about himself and about the monster in him that might one day make her scream again.

"What *did* make you afraid?" he pleaded.

"It doesn't matter," she said. He could hear by her voice that her head was down. "It wasn't there."

"Tell me what it was. Tell me. I will judge."

"It doesn't matter—sir," she said.

"Tell me, Pertelote," Chauntecleer cried, almost angry. "Tell me, so that I never become the thing you fear. Pertelote, I should despair to be the thing that makes you afraid!"

"Lord Chauntecleer!" Pertelote spoke with so much authority—more than that, there was such a choking pain in her voice—that the Rooster swallowed and fell silent. Then she continued: "Lord Chauntecleer, you are something to me. But you're asking me to remember things I don't want to remember. You want me to name a name which suffocates me. I don't want to go back, Chauntecleer. Not even in my mind do I want to go back." She was beseeching him, and leaving pauses in her speech so that he might say something. "I don't want to ruin the peace which your Coop has given me. I don't want to die again."

Then don't, Chauntecleer said in his mind. But he didn't say it out loud, and a long time passed by. Then:

"You looked like Cockatrice." Pertelote breathed the words so very softly, and Chauntecleer began to hate himself.

"I thought there were scales on your stomach; but it was only mud. I thought that I had not gotten away, that there was nowhere in the world to hide—but it was you, with a bleeding wound. And your name isn't Cockatrice. It's Chauntecleer. But I didn't know that, and I screamed. So. So. So."

In the silence that followed Chauntecleer almost didn't breathe. He held himself in utter contempt. He wished that he could hold her now, to comfort her; but at the same time he felt that he had lost that right forever by forcing her—for his own petty foolishness—backward into such an obvious pain. And after all of this, he had not the slightest idea who Cockatrice might be. So it was a worthless triumph. His was a damn hollow victory. In return for a name which meant nothing to him, he had separated himself from the Beautiful Pertelote. In return for what?—a Cockatrice—he had caused her a nameless hurt all over again.

"Lady," he managed to say, scraping the floor with a fat and stupid claw, "I'm sorry."

[74]

She said nothing.

"I'm not even something fearful," he mumbled. "Just cheap."

Still, she said nothing. And that was, he thought, as it should be. But he heard a stirring where she was; and then she came very close to him and laid her head upon his shoulder.

Immediately every thought of apology fled from his brains. Immediately he was breathing very much. Immediately he stretched his wings around her for the second time, and held her tightly, and gurgled.

She had come to him for comfort. Why, then, what a comfort he would be to her! But—now that he wanted them—the poor Chauntecleer had absolutely no words to say. They had all gone away, and he was left with an empty head, all on account of her willing touch. Out of his empty head there stuck a beak; and upon that beak there began to dance a silly smile. He turned his neck, and in the half-light he smiled at everyone in the Coop, one at a time, though every last one of them was sleeping.

And when the river ice exploded its most remarkable gun, a splitting crack which made the Coop to tremble, Chauntecleer thought it to be a most charming and meaningful sound.

So they were married in the snow. It was a snow wedding, for they made their procession through the snow, and the snow fell on them as they went. In the front of a long line of dancing animals, there strutted a proud golden cock and next to him his bride. And the feathers at her throat were a flame so crimson and so intense that they warmed the cock beside her.

"WHEE-YA-HOO!"

This amazing cheer came from the middle of the procession. Animals turned around when they heard it; but when they looked, they couldn't tell for sure who had made it. For in the middle of the procession was Mundo Cani Dog; and, riding on his nose, Tick-tock the Black Ant. Now, Mundo Cani Dog was weeping so helplessly that no one thought the cheer had come from him. And surely the dignified little Ant on the tip of his nose couldn't have . . . wouldn't have . . . But there, on his tiny black face, was a tiny black smile.

In the middle of a white field, all the dancers formed a wide ring around Chauntecleer and his bride. Then they stamped the snow down in special places to write words in it and to draw pictures there. The pictures were blooming flowers, snow lilies and the winter rose. Someone drew a magnificent stallion in the snow, with its mane wild in the wind. Someone else drew the midnight sky and filled it with all of the stars which had not been seen for months. Another one drew a map of Chauntecleer's land, and drew an iron fence all the way around it—to say, This land is protected. Beryl was the last to draw. She came forward shy and delicate, and she drew her picture with much love. When she was done, the entire congregation said, "Ah!" though hers was, perhaps, the simplest drawing of all. Yet it was the most perfect. She had drawn three fair eggs, one beside the other in the snow. Chauntecleer said, "I will name them now." The animals fell silent to listen. "I will name them Ten Pin and Five Pin and One Pin. And they shall all be sons!" The animals cheered, and Chauntecleer burst into joyful laughter. The Beautiful Pertelote put her head down and was happy.

These were the gifts which his animals had brought him on his wedding day. And the words which they wrote in the snow were these:

"OUR LORD AND LADY STAND IN THE EYE OF GOD. LET HIM BE KIND TO THEM."

Here ends the first part of the story about Chauntecleer the Rooter and his Coop, Wyrm's Keepers.

PART TWO

[ELEVEN] Cockatrice rules his land unto its utter destruction

Cockatrice never buried the bones of his father, nor ever again seemed to think of them. Senex lay ragged in his little heap to the left of the Coop door day and night untouched. Blowflies saw an opportunity and took it: They slipped underneath his feathers and massed their tiny yellow eggs by the thousands against his ancient flesh; and when the right time had passed, maggots lived in his body. They ate through his eyes, until Senex was sightless before heaven; they ate his tongue, and Senex was speechless; they squirmed through his old wooden heart; they dwelt in the little sack of his stomach. They were the only life left in the Rooster—and that for but a little while, because Senex had died exhausted, with remarkably little meat on his bones.

A stench arose in the land. The poor animals whined and scraped at their noses. Everywhere they gagged and vomited. Eating became impossible. And the smaller and the weaker among them took sick and began to die. The very smell itself was so oppressive, like grief, that small hearts simply could not bear it and stopped beating. This was no plague, because there were no symptoms with the dying. Incredibly, this was just an odor—foul, thick, blighting, and horribly rotten.

So those animals who could think most clearly formed a committee in order to carry a petition to Cockatrice; they had no other Lord.

They found him not in the Coop. He had not again entered that building after Senex had dropped down dead before it. They found him idle below an enormous Oak which grew near the bank of the river. Next to him was squatting Toad, the same who had brooded over Cockatrice's leathery egg. But neither one greeted the Committee as it approached, nor gave them leave to talk.

"Well," said a Hog, nuzzling the ground, "we have come."

Toad blinked hugely, but silently. Cockatrice merely turned his red eye upon the Hog and slowly twisted his serpent's tail.

"Well," said the Hog again, shifting his barrel weight from side to side, "we have something to say. To *ask*," he hastily caught himself: "To ask."

Low down among the Committee was a Mouse, unnoticed. He was darting his eyes from the Hog to Cockatrice and back again, fiercely anxious that the meeting be neither lost nor wasted.

"Well," said the Hog again; and the Mouse quickly set his teeth, fighting an urge to cut through the Hog's fat obsequiousness and to talk himself. Trees grow slowly. Hogs talk slowly—but they didn't have a whole season now for polite—and stupid—conversation!

"It would be the hon-or-able thing to do"—the Hog snuffled slowly at the ground—"if you, sir, granted your per-mis-sion that we form a pro-ces-sion and take him out of the land, to bury him in some right and distant place. Hon-or-ably, to be sure." The Hog took a moment to overturn a stone. "Lord Senex, we mean," he said.

"No!" The word came in a loud bass voice. Everyone had been looking at Cockatrice, expecting the decision to be his. But he hadn't spoken. He only continued to twist his tail and to regard them all with his red eye as from a great distance. With astonishment everyone glanced from Cockatrice to Toad; and then it was clear that *he* had spoken.

Nevertheless, when the Hog began to speak again, all eyes were back on Cockatrice.

" 'No,' you say," said the Hog. "But surely you un-der-stand custom, and surely you are com-mit-ted to the good purpose of very old custom, and it is our custom to bury our dead. Lord Senex, the Rooster with his Back to the Mountains."

"Custom, crap!" the Mouse cried out suddenly, unable to stand it any longer. "He stinks, and it's killing us!"

"And besides ev-ery-thing else," continued the Hog, "his body is in a state of decay, no fault of his, of course—nor any fault to you, sir."

("Damn!" said the Mouse.)

"He is pu-tre-fying, sir, and you yourself may have no-ticed that he sends up a ter-ri-fic odor, and that odor, if you please, is un-healthy. It is hurting us."

"Killing us! Killing us!" cried the Mouse.

"No!" It was Toad again, burping answers out of his thick throat, while Cockatrice looked on with his mouth closed.

"And so again you say 'No,' " said the Hog. "But per-haps you do not un-der-stand the pe-ti-tion—"

"The body stays where it is. No honorable," burped Toad, "no end to the smell. No burial. Get out of here!"

It was astonishing to see how the members of the com-mittee so easily hunched their shoulders, and turned, and left, each in his own direction; for with that last word the committee had abruptly dissolved, and it was no more. All except for the Mouse. He remained with burning eyes and a vibrating chest, so quickly was he breathing, so full of hatred was he.

"Murderer!" he squeaked at Cockatrice; but Cocka-trice, with one lazy flap of his wings, ascended to a branch in the oak, found a perch, and looked out over the land. "Murderer!" the Mouse shrieked again; and Toad, sud-denly left alone, bounced round to the other side of the tree trunk to hide himself.

From there Toad burped: "You heard Cockatrice. Get out of here!"

After the failure of the committee, the animals of the

[81]

land broke apart. Each began to make his own way in the world. Each family created its own remedies against the terrible, killing stench—but then kept those remedies to itself and grew narrow eyed and suspicious over-against its neighbors. Each family sought its own food, stored it in secret places, then wept in frustration upon finding that the stench would always rot it, wherever it was hidden. But there had to be a blame for such a continuous disaster; so every family blamed the next, with dire threats and menacing looks as they passed one another. The animals of the land descended from speech to snarls, barks, roars, and bleated accusations. And the children, those left living, feared to leave their homes.

Almost as evil as the stench was the silence. Senex, however poorly he had ended his rule, had always remembered the canonical crows. He sang them, to be sure, in a disoriented manner; but he did sing them, keeping his animals that way, banding them, unifying them. But Cockatrice never crowed the canon. So under him the day lost its meaning and its direction, and the animals lost any sense of time or purpose. Their land became strange to them. A terrible feeling of danger entered their souls, of things undone, of treasures unprotected. They were tired all the day long, and at night they did not sleep. And it was a most pitiful sight to see, how they all went about with hunched shoulders, heads tucked in, limping here and there as if they were forever walking into an ill wind, and flinching at every sound as if the wind carried arrows.

And their confusion became dreadful when one day the Mouse ran among them, screaming for them to come and see Senex's body.

"You thought it was one thing," he cried. "But you've got to know! You have to know that it is something else, something worse! Don't blind yourselves! Come and see!"

For the last time in that land, all of the animals did one

[82]

thing together. The Mouse's intensity moved them. Together they went to the Coop and looked.

And Senex was only bones. Dry bones with a scrap of feather here and there. A sad little skull, ribs needle thin, and strange yellow claws—colored as if they alone were left alive. The animals blinked.

"Don't you understand?" the Mouse cried. "Senex doesn't make this stink, and it will not go away with him. Something else makes it. Something else is killing us! And we will be nothing until we find out." He lowered his voice and glared at the ring of animals around the bones and himself. "I'll give you a name," he said. No one encouraged him. No one discouraged him. "The name, *Cockatrice*. The stench came with him. There is nothing left of Senex *to* rot. But Cockatrice sits in his Oak, and the stench remains. He is no Lord. He is an enemy."

At the first mention of Cockatrice, the animals on the outer edge of the circle simply turned and began to walk away; and as the Mouse continued his desperate pleading, the circle shrank altogether—until the Hog was the last to leave. The Mouse skittered after him and bit his leg.

"Damn fools!" he squeaked. "Ignorant, mindless, stupid, sloppy, mad, damn fools!" But the Hog spun on the Mouse, nearly killed him with a snap of his jaws, then lumbered on.

Shaking with frustration, the Mouse turned back to the bones of the old Rooster. Then he saw that one creature yet remained: Toad, hugely blinking his eyes.

"The name of Cockatrice in vain," Toad burped. "Useless, little bitty Mouse. All your chatter—useless. Cockatrice sends me to say: No more meetings. No more gatherings. No more talk among the animals! Hush," whispered Toad, a green foot in front of his mouth as if warning a child. "Hush. Go about your own business and forget the others. Oh, and the Oak, she has a name. She is the Terebinth Oak."

The Mouse shot furiously at Toad; but in three fat hops he had disappeared safely inside the Coop and was gone.

Toad went into the Coop for more than safety. He had a mission there as well.

The hundred Hens sat quietly, each upon her own nest, fearful to move anywhere. The place seemed a most foreboding, dark, uneasy hospital.

"Let me see," burped the pigeon-footed and ugly Toad. When no one offered to let him see anything, he commanded: "In the name of Cockatrice, let me see!" Then he squeezed underneath the nearest Hen. She leaped up with a painful squawk. Three eggs were discovered. Toad broke each of them, then ordered the poor Hen out of the Coop.

This he did with each Hen. Those who were laying he sent out; those who were not stayed in. Finally, the layers in a flock he forced toward the river and the Terebinth Oak, where Cockatrice awaited them.

Cockatrice was not altogether idle, in those days. He wanted children. Hundreds and hundreds, thousands of children; and, almost casually, he ignored the tears and the cries of the Hens, and he went about getting himself children—all in the open, all underneath the Terebinth Oak.

Soon the hens bore the blank look of despair upon their faces. Hope, self-esteem, life itself had been tortured out of them, and they had become feathered machinery, bent to Cockatrice's bloodless will. Cockatrice never looked them in the eyes. He offered nothing for an egg.

And so the space under the Oak was crowded with eggs, waiting to hatch.

For the first time Cockatrice roused himself. Let but one poor animal step too closely to this treasure, and Cockatrice would swoop so suddenly and so wildly from the tree that the creature would die of a faint heart.

Toad spent time moving among and turning the eggs.

"Over, my pretty," he burped motherly. "The sun on your tummy, the sun on your back, to color your coming a poisonous black! I hear you, my pretty. But give it a little time. Time before you hatch." He slept on top of the eggs. Cockatrice never slept.

When the first round of eggs did hatch, the Hens, even in their death walk, were horrified. Some had placed some expectation upon the next generation. Some had even conceived a distorted affection for what Cockatrice had borne upon them. But the creatures which crawled out of these eggs were in no way like chicks. Black, licorice long, damp, each with two burning eyes in its head and teeth already in its mouth, they were small, curled serpents. Basilisks.

Cockatrice swept into the hatching eggs. He roared a greeting which terrified every animal in the land. Then he opened his enormous mouth and swallowed up serpent after serpent. With his throat bulging, he took to the air, flew in great, triumphant circles, writhing his tail frightfully, and then passed low over the river water. There he vomited his brood, and the Basilisks fell like a black rain into the water.

With energy he drove the Hens to produce more and more eggs, even among the shells of the latter ones. He was obsessed; and Toad himself took no more joy in the high office of egg turner, but began to shrink from the watchful red eye above him. Oh, Cockatrice had his children! He had them by the thousands. And again and again he performed the ceremony of a flight and a black rain of Basilisks into the river.

But one Hen, even underneath her agony, kept life within her. She did it by a small plot which she carried out night after night, eternally. She had found a stone the size of an egg, and during the day she sat obediently upon this stone. But when night fell, she would push it to the lower end of her sitting, and then quietly beat herself against the

[85]

stone, slowly, but with force and with pain. Every true egg inside of her she crushed this way before it was laid.

She had a patch of crimson feathers at her throat.

At the beginning of this borning process, it had been Toad's habit at least to chat and banter with the Hens. He played a middle road, doing service for Cockatrice, but at the same time searching for a little forgiveness from the Hens, who were being so sadly used. But the more earnest Cockatrice became about his children, the more irritable Toad became about everything. He was losing place. He, who had brooded Cockatrice into this world, was losing the favor of Cockatrice. Toad wanted something, then— something to win back the favor of his Lord and to prove his importance.

Therefore, he was not silent when he came upon the stone egg.

Toad still examined the Hens, searched their openings to see by the size of them whether this Hen or that one continued to be a layer. This without apology or grace: He crawled underneath them where they sat.

One day he pushed himself out from under the Hen with fire at her throat and began to scream:

"Now, now, here it is!" he cried, hopping among the Hens. "What I was looking for! What I knew would be! Treachery, Cockatrice! Oh, treachery! A stone egg that can never hatch!"

His cry turned Cockatrice's head. It also brought a small Mouse out of the fields.

As soon as Cockatrice was looking, Toad began to hop against the guilty Hen. While she did nothing to protect herself, he fired his fat body like a dumdum at her neck and head, and she began to choke and to cough. "Treachery! Treachery!" cried Toad with every attack.

Immediately the Mouse was there. He fastened his tiny teeth in Toad's face and would not let go. A flurry rippled through the other Hens. A few animals were drawn closer by the screaming.

Toad forgot the Hen. Hop by broken hop, dragging the vicious Mouse with him, he struggled closer to the Terebinth Oak. He cried a new tune:

"Son of my sitting!" he burbled pitifully. "Save me! They're murdering me!"

Not to save the Toad, but for other reasons of his own, Cockatrice opened his mouth and roared like thunder above the noise: "CHILDREN!"

It may have been that, encouraged by the Mouse's fight, some of the gathering animals were considering a fight of their own. Perhaps one creature's spirit could give spirit to the others, and a true revolt might begin. A Black Bear was up on his hind legs, waving his arms with menace. A Wolf was tensing his muscles for a deadly spring. But none of that matters much.

For as soon as Cockatrice roared his order over the land, the river began to boil—hectic churning. Then out of the water, by the thousands, the Basilisks poured. They slimed their way across the land with incredible speed. They shot like arrows among the animals, bit them with poison in their bite, and killed the poor astonished creatures where they stood.

Frantically the Hens exploded away from the Terebinth Oak, and some few survived; but the rest were no match, and they died.

The Mouse was killed at the very trunk of the Oak, for he had not taken his teeth out of Toad's face, and he had not run. But so was Toad killed. Before the Basilisks there was no distinction one from the other.

Then the thousands of Basilisks spread outward from the Oak into all the land, killing and killing every living body they came upon. No animal was prepared to meet such an enemy. None was able to return the fight. Like a black fire the Basilisks ate the land dead until not a soul was left in it, except Cockatrice sitting silently in his tree. The Hog lay down with a single bite in his neck. The Bear with a bite between his toes was cast upon the ground, his

[87]

eyes still open. The Wolf had gone so far as to snap one serpent up; but that serpent had bitten the Wolf on his tongue and then had slithered unharmed out of a dead Wolf's mouth.

No longer was Cockatrice's gaze faraway. This, now, was his business. From the top of the Terebinth Oak he watched the slaughter with attention and with cheer. "Children," he breathed over and over to himself. "Ah, my children."

And from below the ground, from within the prison of the earth, there spoke another, greater voice: *"Circumspice, Domine,"* Wyrm rumbled powerfully, almost peacefully. *"Videat Deus caedem meum."*

"Let God in his heaven witness all my murder," spoken in the language of the powers.

When that land—once under the rule of Senex, the Rooster with his Back to the Mountains—had become a sepulcher and a wilderness with the dead lying everywhere, then the Basilisks withdrew again into the river. Then Cockatrice himself—in his own good time—left the place. He took to his mighty wings and flew west, for so the river flows.

And then it began to rain on earth.

[Twelve] *The rains*

he wasted land, the shattered society, the bodies dead and festering, were all great Wyrm's triumph. In one small part of the earth his Keepers had been first weakened and then killed. Their lives, which locked his life beneath them in the earth; their banded peace, which chained him there; their goodly love, which was his torment; their righteousness, which was iron against his will—that fabric had in one place on the earth been torn.

So one part of the earth's crust was softened, and Wyrm rejoiced. Could he but spread that soft, vulnerable area across a continent and to the sea, then he could himself blast through the crust, break free, and gallop through the spheres of the universe. Oh, he would swallow the moon in a gulp. He would bloody the sun. And he would roar almighty challenges to the Lord God Himself. He would spew chaos among the stars; and he would whirl his tail with such power that when it hit the earth, that planet would be cracked from its fixed position at the center of things to spin like nonsense going nowhere. While Cockatrice flew westward above, Wyrm dreamed dreams below: He himself would make of his earth prison a puny mockery. *He* would make it little among the planets and nothing among the suns. *He* would snatch purpose from its being, giving it a loose, erratic, meaningless course to travel. *He* would surround it with cold, empty space. And *he* would cancel heaven from above it.

Oh, how Wyrm hated this round ball, the earth! How he yearned to be out of it forever, to see it a piece of dust, whimpering from the edge of a galaxy for its God!

[89]

Therefore, when the Lord God saw that the land just west of the mountains had fallen to Wyrm's deceit, God himself cloaked the entire earth in cloud. He shut it up. Sadly, he closed it from the rest of creation, and he left it to other Keepers to keep Wyrm imprisoned.

That was when the rains began.

So, although he could not know it, it was a very lonely rain which fell on Chauntecleer the day he sat alone upon his mud heap in an empty field. And the clouds that covered his first meeting with the Beautiful Pertelote—they were God's doing. And the war which he was about to fight—it was of tremendous significance.

One thing the Lord God did do for his Keepers, that they be not altogether alone in the struggle to come: He sent his messenger to them. The Dun Cow, her eyes so full of compassion, appeared in Chauntecleer's land to speak a word or two.

Yet, despite these convulsions above and below him, Chauntecleer the Rooster pottered through his life in regular Rooster fashion, enjoying his marriage and looking toward the spring. He could do that simply because he was ignorant of matters greater than his Coop. Perhaps that was good. Perhaps not. In either case, that's the way that it was.

[Thirteen] *The spring, with foreblessing and foreboding*

ecause something fell out of the sky daily, even into the spring, the winter snow left with a weird speed that year. It had heaped itself so monumentally across Chauntecleer's land that the Coop had finally been sitting in a deep, white scallop. But then, between a night and a day, snowfall turned to drizzle and mist. The mist froze at a touch upon the snow, which, for a night and a day, had the smooth, shining, and eerie shapes of ice on top of it. Another night and another day, and the ice was etched and gouged by channels of racing water, and the Coop withstood a perilous splashing. Then thunderstorms broke the weather: growling first in the east, striding by wide thunder steps toward the Coop, then suddenly cracking asunder the sky and the earth with wild, stuttering lightning. And that was it for the snow. But the water yet flowed everywhere.

Southeastern winds met the west winds over Chauntecleer's land, and the storms produced were lasting and savage.

The Rooster would hear an electric *zzzz*, like a sigh from the points of twigs and old grass; his feathers would rise a fraction on their own; then—*CRACK!* Blue, dazzling light; a ripping of elements; and the frightful thunder went slamming into everything that stood upright. The storm strode on brilliant, quivering spiders' legs all around his Coop; and the rain drove at the earth as if it were intent on digging craters. The Hens huddled, and the Rooster crowed his canonical crows with particular

[91]

care and assurance; for his soul knew well where the sun was, though the sun was hidden and never showed itself: Chauntecleer's crowing had *become* both sunlight and certitude for his animals; it made for them the day they never saw. It pointed placement for all their scattered and shredded feelings. And it brought them through in good order.

Because, finally, the storms strode westward and away—and a gentle spring was given her time in spite of the sky's confusion.

Spring: The moist air smelled of loam and the earth. It smelled like flowers even before the flowers had begun to bloom. Chauntecleer had preserved hope in his animals during the storms; so when the storms left, the animals quickly forgot them. And when the new spring air filled up with sweetness and promises, so very quickly the hearts of the Hens were stirred. They clucked, gossiped, joked, giggled, and grinned; they swept the floor with feathered brooms, scrubbed the roosts, poked at cobwebs, dusted with down, and threw every window wide open. Spring! The air puffed through the open Coop and gently tugged at the feathers on their backs. And that was a good feeling. The busy waters outside chuggled and laughed gladly. And that was a good sound. Seven young Mice and three young Chicks tumbled joyfully through the Coop, squealing and falling over each other; and thirty-one Hens didn't mind their games at all.

That was a good time.

Lord Russel, the Fox of Good Sense, had taken to visiting the Coop often these days; and then who fussed at him or shooed him away? Nobody. They welcomed the blatherer, even listened to his many stories of clever escapes— and listened so well, with so many appreciative clucks, that he decided to reveal unto them several marvelous tricks known only to himself and to his grandfather, long since dead. And while he explained the finer intricacies of his tricks, the three young Chicks—named Ten Pin, Five Pin, and One Pin—sat down in wonder and gaped.

"Children, to be sure, of their father," the Fox would say. "The spitting—not to say *spitting*—images of the old crow, *er*, Cock. But it is rather more evident, more to the point, *most* evident, that they possess, each one of them, the uncommon acumen, the, shall we say, uncommon Good Sense of their uncle. *Ahem!* Shrewd uncle"—by which he was, of course, referring to himself. For he had decided that any Chick who took such an interest in his arcane tricks should be nephew to him. And here there were, Glory be!, three such Chicks! Therefore he would be without discrimination an uncle to all three of them. The Fox took Pins One, Five, and Ten under his wing, so to speak, and came to the Coop exceedingly often.

It was a very good time!

Even Mundo Cani Dog looked around the Coop from where he lay in front of the door and found it possible to grin a cavernous and toothy grin. Once somebody heard him laugh. But then a debate developed on whether the Dog had really laughed after all. Neither side triumphed in the debate, for nobody heard him laugh again. But there sat that smile on his continent of a face, and that was good for something.

John Wesley Weasel sat himself down at Ebenezer Rat's old exit at the back of the Coop and did an astonishing thing: Moved by the spring, he was striking up a relationship with the Wee Widow Mouse. "Sparking," he called it. "Sparking the Widow."

"Mice cleans in the spring," he said through the hole, while the Widow hunched and puttered over her cleaning. "I see. That I see. John Double-u understands. Mice and Double-u's is different, there's a fact. Look different—on account of Mice is squeaky homebodies. Double-u's is beings of the whole outdoors. Nothing to a Double-u to spend a whole night outside a-huntin'. Bring home food for the family, you understand. For the family, you understand." He looked significantly into the Widow's home to see if she understood, to see whether she had taken the true depth of his meaning. "Look different. Double-u's got finer fur and sleekier backs and twistier turnings. Run at a clip and fight like the devil. Double-u's takes care of their own. Is well able to take care of their own. Of their own, you understand." He looked significantly at the Widow. He was sparking, you understand. "So Mice cleans in the spring. Well, now. There's a marvel. There's a habit I could learn to"— here John Wesley had a small coughing fit—"like."

And the Ants came marching seven by seven, carrying enormous quantities of food to their hole, where the larder had grown bare: Corn kernels and dead beetles thirteen times their size they carried. "HUP, WHO, HREE, HOR!" Tick-tock marched at the head of the column, crying commands. "WHA ARE WE FOR?" And a chorus of rumbling bass voices sang in return: "BUSY-NESS AND WORK, *SIR*! NEVER WILL WE SHIRK, *SIR*!"

"Morning, morning, cousin Chauntecleer," Tick-tock said as they passed by the Rooster. "A fine and likely morning you have crowed in. Propitious for a little bit of doing."

Chauntecleer didn't answer. But Tick-tock had only spoken out of the corner of his mouth, too busy to notice the look in the Rooster's face, and he marched on.

It was a very good time, the springtime.

But as it progressed, and as the waters giggled running away, Chauntecleer the Rooster acted more and more strangely. Sometimes he was with his animals, laughing louder, strutting prouder and grinning broader than any of them. At such times he knew what the spring was about and, in spite of the lasting rain, he enjoyed its promises with all of his heart. But at other times a strained, worried look came into his eyes; and then, no matter what good thing was going on around him, he grew silent and went inside of himself. Then he didn't answer his animals' questions, and he didn't notice when they were telling jokes. Then he ate very little. And he began to take trips by himself. He would disappear from the Coop without a word for hours at a time, returning heavy with mud and heavy with worry. When the trips lasted throughout an afternoon, and then when they began to stretch out into a full day, the animals heard terce, sext, and none crowed in a tiny triple Peep.

"The Pins," they would say; and they would nod to one another.

Chauntecleer had two separate feelings going on inside of him that spring. They were like two worms in his soul, and they were fighting with each other, first one winning and then the other. One worm was good, nearly a butterfly. This was the feeling which he got from the Beautiful Pertelote, from the three Pins, his children, and from the joyful, springtime Coop.

No one had ever heard him crow lauds as he crowed lauds these early mornings! Oh, he reared back his head, threw out his chest, flustled his feathers as if they were a shimmering army, and let fly with a full cannonade of a crow: "COCK-A-WING-DING-DOOOOO! GOD BLESS THE WORLD AND *YOU*!" Then he was proud, was dizzy with pride. For he stood on the haunch of a mountainous Dog, and there beside him stood three young Chicks— their yellow heads back, their yellow chests out, their yellow, downy feathers making an awful effort to bristle.

"PEEP!" they cried, and Chauntecleer fell down off the Dog and rolled laughing on the ground.

Three Chicks thought that this was wonderful; so they pipped-pipped-PEEPED all over again. And their father laughed until his stomach hurt and he got the hiccups.

"Congratulations, twits," he roared. "God put trumpets in your throats! Why, you will blast the morning from

[95]

her mooring and shatter the east! Peep? Ah-ha-ha-ha!"
And he kicked at the air in his joy.

Pins One, Five, and Ten jumped onto his chest, and he
knocked them away like cotton balls. Then he gathered
them together under his wing and said, "Ye are lions,
roaring lions, and sons to me."

The Beautiful Pertelote saw these things from the doorway and was glad.

But then she saw what no one else was seeing. She saw
the look of worry tug at Chauntecleer's eyes—until he
grew silent, and set his Pins up in a straight, proud row,
and went off on another private trip.

The other feeling in his soul during this springtime was
an eating, unsatisfied worm. It chewed at him and made
him restless. It wouldn't let him sleep at night, or else it
invited dreams not good. It made him to be what he had
never thought he would be again: lonely. He forgot that
he could talk to Pertelote, and she didn't remind him; for
in her love she let him be.

Chauntecleer's trips were to the river. It was the river
which was confusing and troubling him. And more than
that, it was what he thought he saw there which made him
so private in his anxiety.

The river had never stopped its swelling. During the
previous winter it had, certainly, frozen; but even the ice
had not locked it in its place. Rather, it had continued to
swell until it burst through that coat of iron ice, like a
living, serpentine monster splitting open its shell, and
great chunks of ice went spinning away in the current. The
ice would form again; the river would swell again, more
than before; and again the ice would break above the
strain. All winter this had gone on, the river growing and
growing; and Chauntecleer had gone to watch its growth
and to worry. He worried because he did not understand
it. He no longer recognized his borderland river.

And he worried profoundly because he had begun to
see visions.

For example, when he looked at the ice chunks in the river, they became heads even while he was looking— heads bobbing up and down in the water. At first they were no more than heads, with their mouths and their eyes closed, mute, expressionless. And they were all of them white. They looked to him like the heads of lions, or of cows; they were wolves and bears and lambs and bulls, calves and kids. Once Chauntecleer thought that this was a trick of his eyes, and he might have let it pass. But as he had gone back again and again through the winter, the ice had always poured by as severed heads. And when their eyes opened up and began to look back at him, then he knew that it was no trick, but a vision he was having, and he waited to learn something from the vision. He continued to return. Yet the heads taught him nothing. They looked at him with deep sorrow in their eyes. Presently the mouths, too, opened up; and the Rooster heard the sounds of grief in his vision. Bawling and bleating, sobbing and keening, the heads flowed by him in the river; but never a word did they speak. Chauntecleer returned troubled.

And now the spring had come. The heads had melted away, and the Rooster's vision was over. But the worm in his soul was not gone; for still the river had not stopped its swelling.

The river was a flood—as it had never been before. And, boiling far beyond its banks, the flood picked up every floating thing on either side of it, rushing each thing away in its current. The good river had become a destruction, silently swallowing Chauntecleer's land foot by foot. It scoured the earth away from the roots of the trees. It pressed against these trees until they collapsed; and then it rushed them away as well. It swallowed nearby hills, creeping ever closer to the Coop. Miles are miles; miles are a long way to go, and so it was not yet anywhere near the Coop. But there came a day, during this spring, when Chauntecleer left the three Pins behind him in a proud,

[97]

straight row and went to look at the river's flood. On this day his worry slipped very close to panic, because when he looked he could not see the other side. Water covered all the land to the south as far as he could see; and what is more, the water was not still. It sucked and snuffled at the edges of the earth with its boiling current.

And that night poor Chauntecleer had a dream.

[FOURTEEN] *Chauntecleer's dream, the first engagement with the enemy*

his was not a dream which comes *out* of the dreamer. It was the kind of dream which goes *into* him. And so it came with a hard power. And so its ending was neither fixed nor determined by its beginning. Some dreams are merely pockets in sleep, to be filled up with things from the sleeper's memory, and they pass with the waking. Others become solid events in the dreamer's life, sleeping *or* awake. Chauntecleer's dream was of the second kind.

He dreamed that he was standing on a small, muddy island in the middle of the river. There was room for his standing but no more. The river stretched all around him till, in every direction, it merged with the grey sky; and there was not a twig or a leaf to be seen anywhere. But it *was* the river, for it had a current and his island made the water gutter and ripple.

The water stank with such a loathsome odor that the Rooster could not breathe without gagging. The rotten smell was strangling him. He was shaking his head violently to be rid of it, but to no good.

And it seemed to him at the beginning of his dream that he was waiting for somebody. He was angry that he had to wait so long in such a place.

"Why don't they come?" he said in a gagging voice.

"Pax, Galle superbe," the river answered him in the language of the powers. But in his dream Chauntecleer was

neither surprised by the river's talk nor ignorant of its meaning. It seemed natural, and he understood it: "Peace, Proud Chauntecleer," the river kindly hummed to him. "I know your trouble, and I have remembered you with an island out of my own bosom. I know your distress, and I shall companion you. I am both your company and your haven, Proud Chauntecleer. Peace."

But Chauntecleer was angry.

"I don't want your island," he snapped. "Flush your island! I want them here, and I need them now. Oh, why don't they come?"

"By now, dear Chauntecleer, you should have learned how quicksilver are the hearts of those you serve. Yesterday's gratitude is forgotten today. Forgive me my speaking the truth," sang the river mildly, "but their need once satisfied, they do forget the Lord who led them, and then he's left alone—his own need and himself, alone. They have forgotten you, lonely Chauntecleer."

"I don't believe it! They will come!"

"And as for my island, consider how very much you need it. Consider flight, should I withdraw it from you— though I mean no such threat—and wonder whither you might fly. Consider the unutterable loneliness should I fall silent and cease to speak with you—"

"You see?" the Rooster suddenly cried out. "Look there! You see? They're coming for me! They haven't forgotten!" Chauntecleer leaped and waved at a dark spot on the horizon.

"No, rather *you* shall see, Proud Chauntecleer. And then *you* shall know the truth."

As it drew nearer, the spot showed as a boat made out of branches. Then it was a whole series of boats, a fleet, and the animals who rode them were his own. Chauntecleer grinned and forgot his anger. "Ha, ha!" he laughed, and prepared to leave the island. "Here I am! Here I am! I knew you wouldn't forget me!"

Silently the first boat swept toward the Rooster; silently

it breasted him, and silently it passed by. Pins One, Five, and Ten had not so much as looked at him.

"Pertelote!" Chauntecleer cried to the passenger on the second boat, "drag the water and turn. Or look at me! Just look at me!"

But the second boat passed with the first.

"Oh, thankless breed of creatures," sang the river.

"Shut up! Shut up!" shouted the Rooster, suddenly desperate.

"We shall see," the river sang calmly.

"Here!" cried Chauntecleer to the Weasel on the third boat. "I'm over here. You can swim, John. I can't. Steer here! Here! Here!"

But one after the other the boats passed the island; and none paused, nor would anyone on the boats glance at the screaming Rooster standing on it: the Wee Widow Mouse and her children; Beryl, Chalcedony, and twenty-eight Hens in grim procession.

"Stop! Give me a ride! Oh, save me!" Chauntecleer pleaded with Mundo Cani—first to his blank face, and then to his back. It was a humiliation that Chauntecleer should have to plead with the Dog at all; but it was wasted humility. The Dog sailed away with the others.

"I hate you!" Chauntecleer screamed at the disappearing boats. "Hate you! Hate you! Hate you all!"

His throat hurt with the screaming. And when he was alone again his chest convulsed with angry sobs. But, strangely in this dream, it felt very good to be screaming these words, and the sobs were sweet medicine. Chauntecleer had much pity for himself, lost and ignored upon his island. But the self-pity, too, felt good. It was a comfort and a relief and even a baneful sort of triumph to be screaming pure hatred from the bottom of his soul—especially when he felt that he had the *right* to hate. They had done him first! Therefore his was righteous wrath, deserved self-pity.

"Ah, so we see the truth," the river hummed mildly all

around him. "We have clear eyes, now, and nothing is hidden from us anymore, and we have become as wise as God. Their Lord provides them comfort in their need. Their lonely Lord fills them with good things, and they answer his benevolence with what? With a cold and bitter distance! With 'Sir' and 'Please you, sir.' Am I right? And then, when the need is *his*—how then, Proud Chauntecleer? What then? Why, foul ingratitude! Oh, proper bird, how lonely you must be!"

"Hate them. Hate them," Chauntecleer mumbled, savoring the pain. "Hate them all."

"Aye! They, the *ingrati*." The river began to toll terrible words, naming the Rooster's animals for him. "And they, the *oblivii*. And they, the *peccati*. Here I have remembered you, and with an island out of my own bosom have saved you alive. But they have forgotten you, turned away from you, cut you off, despised you, sentenced you to misery and a forsaken death. *Ingrati! Oblivii! Peccati!*"

Though they were spoken in a quiet manner, Chauntecleer knew them to be poisonous words, filled with cursing in the language of the powers. The river was offering them to him as if they had been dishes or weapons. The river was inviting him. And so hot was the hatred in the Rooster's soul that he chose one of the river's words, and put it into his own mouth, and said it: *"Ingrati!"* Chauntecleer said.

Immediately the dark spot was on the horizon again, and he saw it. For the second time the boats were coming around.

At the sight Chauntecleer's stomach lurched, and he didn't know what to do. Swiftly they sailed to him where he stood. Would he call to them a second time? Would he humiliate himself again? Or would he stand proud in his lonely silence and let them pass by forever?

But when they drew near to his island, he saw a horror.

Each passenger on each boat lay dead. The Beautiful Pertelote, and all his Hens, dead; John Wesley Weasel, Lord Russel, the Widow and all her children, Mundo Cani, Tick-tock—every one of them dead.

"Then they are well punished for their ingratitude and for your enforced loneliness," the river sang. "Such is my gift to you, Lord Chauntecleer. Receive it with my benediction."

But the Rooster was staring at this procession with a killing guilt. He felt sick with his guilt, because he had said that he hated them. He wanted to die because of his guilt.

Suddenly he began to slap the water with his wings.

"You! You! You!" he screamed, but there was no goodness in the screaming now. "It's you that I hate, you damned of God!"

At once the island started to sink. The water rose up to his legs, and he could not see where he was standing. In his dream it seemed as if he were standing on nothing, surrounded in every direction by the river's water. Yet he shrieked until his voice burst: "I don't care! Dying is little enough for me! Dying is right for me! It's you that I hate!"

"I could cause the island to grow," sang the river. "I could make an Eden of it."

But the Rooster wept for guilt and screamed the louder: "It's you that I hate! I will fight you! Kill me now—right now! Or I will fight you! Fight you! Fight you!" And then, just before he drowned, he cried out: "Oh, Pertelote!"

Pertelote—the real Pertelote—grabbed Chauntecleer in her two wings and shook him. He woke up.

"Chauntecleer, Chauntecleer," she said. She had been saying it over and over. "Chauntecleer. Oh, Chauntecleer, you're dreaming."

For a long, long time that night the Rooster simply let himself be held, his head sagging—and he was grateful. He panted heavily. He swallowed often.

[103]

Then, for a moment, he left Pertelote alone. He stepped down from his perch and went to each of the other creatures in his Coop. One at a time he touched them. When he had touched them, he said their names over to himself. "Beryl. Chalcedony. Chrysolite. Sardonyx. Topaz. Jasper. Jacinth. Emerald. Mundo Cani. And my children; oh, my children." They slept on, so gently had he touched them; and they did not know that he was whispering their names with love.

Pertelote alone knew.

When he was beside her again he spoke. "I will never dream again."

"Can you choose not to dream?" she said.

"I can choose against evil," Chauntecleer said. "I can surely choose against evil, and my dreams have been filled with evil. It's what *I* do in them. And then it's what *I* bring out of them into this place. . . . If I have to stay awake forever, I will never dream again. Yes! I *choose* not to dream."

Pertelote considered the tone of her husband's voice. It was different from what it had been, and so she said, "Will you talk now, Chauntecleer?"

"Oh," he said, truly turning to her, "I never stopped talking."

"Will you answer me a question?"

"Of course. I'm okay now."

But Chauntecleer didn't understand that the difficulty of the question wasn't in him, but in her. When someone seldom talks about herself, she believes that everyone else is like her and that no one wants to talk about himself. But she asked her question:

"Why have you been worried for so long?"

Then Chauntecleer didn't help her in her difficulty. Instead of answering, he gave her question for question:

"Where did you come from, Pertelote?"

She was quiet and didn't answer.

"Shush, shush," he gentled her as if she *had* said something. "My question is as important as yours; they are the
same question, Pertelote. Listen to me: You came to my
land by the river, and so you have something to do with
it, more than I know; and I need to know. Because it is the
river that has worried me for so long. It's flooded the
entire south territory of my land—a strange, unholy flood.
But maybe you can tell me of its source. Maybe you can
teach me something so that I can understand this thing.
Why did you come here, Pertelote?"

"I, too, can choose against evil," she said in a little
voice.

"Then we are one," he said.

"I lived in the land just west of the mountains."

"So far away?"

"It is a long river."

"Longer than I know."

"But I can choose against evil as well as another," Pertelote repeated, for it was important to her that Chauntecleer understand this before she told him her story. If she
was to reveal the vulgar secret of her past, it must be on
her own terms. She must not lose his love in the telling;
and she must not, by his deeper knowledge of her, begin
to hate herself.

Chauntecleer said, "I know your heart, Pertelote. That
I know very well, and it is good."

So then she told him of her land; of Senex, the
Rooster with his Back to the Mountains; of his death
and of the miraculous birth of his child. She told him,
and Chauntecleer learned, of the being who bore the
name *Cockatrice*—his tormenting of the Hens, his children the Basilisks, his destruction of the whole land.
And then she stopped, and the night was quiet again.

Finally Chauntecleer spoke. "Pertelote, Pertelote," he
said. "Not less, but so much more do I love you now."

Having heard her tale, he was calm and deeply happy;

[105]

and he was confident that he would never dream again. What she had told him had not caused this peace, though he had listened well to it. But that she had spoken these things at all in his presence—that critical gesture was his assurance: It pleaded her love and her absolute trust in him. Why, she had placed her very heart into his keeping, believing that he would not harm it. And by heaven, he would not!

[FiFTEEN] Now it begins—sorrow befalls Chauntecleer's land

n the morning every animal stepped out of the Coop—or else rushed toward the Coop—and rejoiced: The rain had stopped falling! For the first time in three seasons the air was clear, and a feather could expect to stay dry the whole day through. Oh, the clouds still covered the earth, and the sun still remained a mystery; but it was a high covering, now—pale, not glowering; luminous, not gloomy; more a white sheet than the melancholy blanket which it had been for so long.

So the animals took a holiday. They gathered, ate, laughed, and danced a step or two. Picnics happened everywhere. Excursions to hunt for mushrooms (thousands and thousands of mushrooms that year) were formed in the blink of an eye. A Dog ambled out of the Coop and breathed through his nose. A Rooster crowed lauds as it had never been crowed before. (Chauntecleer was made joyful by the dry weather, to be sure; but more than that, his talk the previous night with the Beautiful Pertelote had done away with loneliness—and *that* was a joy unspeakable.) And a Weasel suffered seven little Mice to join him in a hunt. ("Is no talking! Is no running! Is no crowding John! A leaf—don't step on it. A hole—God's sake, don't fall in. File single! Noses up, tails down, eyes bright—*faugh!* Listen: Maybe baby Mice rather stay to home. No? No? *Faugh!*")

But what truly gave the day the special feeling of a holiday was that Tick-tock the Black Ant had given his workers the day off.

"LAUDS TO TERCE: GAMES.
TERCE TO SEXT: EXERCISES.
SEXT: DINNER.
SEXT TO NONE: REST,"

he announced. "Ready—begin!"

He marched the troops to the door of the Coop.

"Halt, two, three, four. Games, two, three, four!"

Properly he knocked on the door. Graciously he requested that the Three Pins come out and play a game with them—and the Pins came in a flash, bouncing and rolling over twenty serious Ants before Tick-tock could bark them into order.

"Games!" he said significantly, as if such imprudent bouncing had no place in holidays.

Then the Ant sought a good stream of water (there were so many about); had his workers trundle three chips of wood from the forest to the water; commanded his workers to form three chains of Ants, one from each wood chip to the dry land; suggested the Pins climb on—and, lo, they began to play their game. They gave the Pins rides, pulling them on little boats upstream.

As the Ants always worked to a shouted rhythm, so they also *played* to rhythm. Tick-tock selected the right song for the game; and, with enormous bass voices, the boatmen chanted the chorus:

"On chips of wood the Three Pins sail,
With a puff and a blow and away they go!
The breeze, it rocks them like a gale,
With a wash and a woe—as the rivers flow,
They'll never be home for tea."

Ten Pin looked happily about himself and grinned. It was a good world to be in. It was good to be one whose father was Lord of the land, good to be met with respect and honor, good to be remembered by the Ants. Earnestly they pulled him. Properly they rocked the boat when their song said that something *did* rock the boat. Then they clucked their tiny tongues, as if they had treated the children to wild excitement. Ten Pin only wished that they might go a little faster. When little Ants are cautious, it is a vast caution for big Chicks: The boat was hardly moving.

> "To west, to west, across the sea,
>> *With a puff and a blow and away they go!*
> Three ships, three sailors brave and wee,
>> *With a wash and a woe—as the rivers flow,*
>> *They'll grieve their mother and me."*

Well, the game was becoming a little boring. Anytime Ten Pin rocked the boat on his own, Tick-tock gave him severe looks until the child sat down again.

They had crept three inches up the water, the Black Ant popping his eyebrows up and down as if to say, "Isn't this fun?" Well, thought Ten Pin to himself, fun. Lord Russel, on the other hand, had promised his nephews LARGE-SIZED games, dreadful escapes, things true to life. So then, how could he leave the Ants for something better without hurting their feelings?

> "One lost at sea, one drowned on lee,
>> *With a puff and a blow and away they go!*
> And one still sinking silently,
>> *With a wash and a woe—as the rivers flow,*
>> *They'll not be home for tea, for tea,*
>> *They'll never be home for tea."*

"Stop!" screamed a voice from within the Coop. "Evil tongues! Evil tongues! Not another word from your evil tongues!" Beryl exploded from the door, spilling feathers everywhere in her fury. She drove straight toward Tick-

[109]

tock, her head pumping, her wings whirring, and jabbed the tip of her beak into his face.

"What in the name of everything good are you doing?"

"Halt, two, three, four," Tick-tock called, and the slow boats stopped. "No harm to them, madam," the Ant announced, staring coldly at the Hen in front of him. "Games most respectfully played."

"Games? Disasters! Incantations! Children could drown, for all your games!"

"I beg your pardon. They may damp a feather or two, but they will not drown in a stream stone deep."

"You play reckless! You're foolhardy with the children of my heart!"

"Madam," Tick-tock said with brittle offense, "I took every particular precaution with these children. I am not of a foolhardy nature."

"Stuff! Stuff!" Beryl cried directly into the Ant's face; then she choked up before the wooden stupidity, the insensibility, of the ruffian, and she could say no more. Tick-tock, for his part, wondered about the Hen's sanity.

And for just a moment Ten Pin was delighted. This game seemed soon to be over, and another, better one could begin. To help matters along he began to cough as if a little water had gotten into his lungs.

But his hopes died quickly.

"Spells!" Beryl managed to splutter. "Enchantments!"

Tick-tock only shook his head before this display.

Gingerly, Beryl bumped the Pins from their boats with the tip ends of her wings, as if each one of them were red hot, then brushed them into a yellow heap. In the damp ground around them she scratched a circle with her beak. Then she beat her wings at the Ants. "Words curse, don't you know?" she cried. The Ants stood stolidly by. "No more sense in your tiny black brains than slugs—to be handling *words*, to be light with *words*, and at the children's expense! Oh, to be talking such things!" And, as the Ants never blinked an eye, moved, or even broke their chains, Beryl rushed away to find Chauntecleer.

The Ant delivered himself of an opinion. "Daft," he said. "Words are nothing. Work is all. And that, men," he said, turning suddenly to the rest of them, "is quite enough of holiday madness. Take a lesson: When duty is laid aside for play, troubles arise. Let's get back to work."

And they did. In an instant, and with great relief, the Ants marched away. And then somebody was, after all, busy on the holiday.

Beryl dearly loved the Pins. She had been proud at their birth. She had been proud at the size of them and the speed with which they learned. And she had burst with pride to be chosen their nurse. No one knew how often she stole to their nests of a night, merely to hear their breathing and to assure herself that they were at peace. No one knew how deeply her heart yearned for them each time they went out of her sight—and for that reason she had never permitted them to leave the yard around the Coop. Did they want something from the forest? Well, then, *she* troubled herself to go and get it, whatever it happened to be. Great was her heart for the children, and great her care for them.

Beryl also had an abiding respect for words. As far as she was concerned, the word for a thing somehow *was* that thing. Therefore she never spoke frivolously what she did not mean to say; and she surely never put into words anything which she did not wish to happen. For the words themselves could trigger it, and then it would happen. To say something was to send the thing itself out into the world and out of her control. It was to curse. She never analyzed this faith of hers; she merely believed it and, with a dreadful care, acted accordingly.

Under her breath she prayed blessings upon the heads of the Pins continually. Continually? Why, she had never *ceased* to pray for them since their birth. With words she

[111]

was constructing a defense around them, against danger, against disease, against ill will, against misfortune. All alone, in the secret of her soul, she was building their peace and their good growth—and that with *words.*

But now, despite all her careful spinning, this blind, wretched Ant decides that he shall play a game with the children of her heart. Well and good. She permitted the game. *But not the song!* She did not know that they were going to sing a song over the Pins, a chant which lightly predicted death by drowning for the Pins. What did the fools think they were doing? A game? Oh, Lord God— mischance! Disaster! They had set the children in harm's way!

So Beryl hurried to find Chauntecleer. And she found him in the Coop. But he, too, was slow to understand the Hen's distress.

"A crow, please, sir," she pleaded with him. "A prayer for the safety of your sons."

"Why?" Chauntecleer was startled that such a day as this one should need such a crow as that. "Are they sick? Hurt? Has anyone threatened them?" He stood up, ready to go.

"Not as yet sick nor hurt. Threats, sir, perhaps—"

"Who?"

"No one, sir, but—"

"No one! Threats fall from the sky these days?"

"Well, but there could come the threat. The Ants, you see, have made your sons unsafe."

"How?"

Chauntecleer's fired questions did not help the Hen any, and she was at mortal pains to state her fears clearly. While she tried, and while she wrung her wings before him, the Rooster sat down again and assumed an air both lordly and knowing in front of her. All of this, of course, took time; and the nervous Hen, starting and stopping in her explanation, glancing from the door to the Rooster, stumbled often as she spoke.

[112]

And so it was that, for the first time in their young lives, the Three Pins were left utterly alone, their nurse and then their tiny playmates having left them. Ten Pin immediately saw the treasure of the opportunity. By a judicious use of his own words, he persuaded his brothers to join him in adventure; and gingerly—as gingerly as Beryl had herself set them there—they stepped over the line of the circle. Then they skittered like water bugs over the yard, out of the yard, and into the forest.

Ten Pin laughed as if his heart would break. He was free!

"Well. So. And then, yes. Indeed, it is a trick which I have been saving until a special time. And this, Nephews, I propose—this is a special time. Mark it: The air is dry. What do you say to that? And besides all that, the air is not wet. Holiday, you see. Special day. And judging by the halcyon qualities—not to say expansive qualities—of your father's canonical crows, this morning, I believe—that he believes—that this is a special time. Personally, that is to say, speaking from my own view of the matter," said the Fox of Good Sense, "I am persuaded that now is a special time—because now is the, er, *right* time!" And he paused to smile, satisfied that he had presented remarkable proofs to shore his argument; he was much learned in rhetoric.

Lord Russel was sitting near his hole in the forest. The Three Pins were sitting in front of him, cuffing one another with glee, giggling, and smelling adventure. So wide was their world! Wider than ever they had imagined. So high went the trees, now that they sat at the roots of them. So wise was their uncle. Just look at the eyes on him!— slanted, with a yellow rheum in the corners, signifying (so he himself had told them) much thought and many sights seen.

"Peep," said Ten Pin aloud, wriggling with expectation. He could hardly keep his tummy still.

"To be sure," cried the Fox. "There is wise counsel in your peep. It is the right time to, as we say, present you with this trick, that is to say, make a present of this trick to you, because it has only just become the summer, er, time."

"Peep."

"*Er*, yes: peep. To be sure. This trick is most effective in the summertime, for it is with the summertime that one begins to experience a mild, albeit irritating and painful, but mild, discomfort. Nephews: fleas! Fleas! And fleas are what this particular trick is about. Therefore, now is the time!"

No matter that the Pins would never get fleas.

"Peep!" Ten Pin cried, beside himself at the revelation that this trick was about fleas. "Peep! Peep!" Pins Five and One clapped their stubby wings.

"Now. Then," began the Fox of Good Sense, cutting through the clamor. "How does one deliver himself of the flea? One cannot, *er*, beat it away from oneself; for in that case one would be beating oneself."

The Pins shouted their laughter at that picture. But the Fox took no notice.

"One could, perhaps, pluck one's hair—*er*, feathers— until one had rendered himself naked from the nave to the, *er*, chaps. And then one might actually *see* the flea in order to chase him all up and down one's, *ahem*, spine—"

How the Pins roared! Oh, how they loved their uncle!

"But in the *first* place," he continued, his eyes faraway, "the flea is a sinister, quick critter, well capable of running faster than one may turn his neck to pounce. Welts, then, may be raised. Scabs produced, and tremendous spasms of the muscles endured. Devilish, devilish, the flea! And in the, *er, second* place, it is a painful operation and time-consuming—that is, to pluck one's hair. And then there is a *third* place, some, *um*, where. So then, these failing, how does one deliver himself of the flea? More to the point, how does one remove from his hide *many* fleas? Ah, by a trick. One must know the Trick of the Stick!"

"But you said," said Ten Pin, suddenly having second thoughts, "that there's no beating."

"A careful and most critical objection, Pin the Tenth. Yet, please understand, *ahem*, that this is not a stick for beating. No, sir. It is a stick of trickery! Your uncle, mind you, is a Fox. Shrewdish he is; brutish he is, *er*, not!"

Lord Russel paused to smile. He was taking note of his joke before launching into his explanation of the Trick of the Stick. And then, with much windy groaning, that is what he did: He launched.

The trick was not at all a bad one, but clever. Russel's reputation had some substance to it.

One found for himself a stick which was at least the length of one's own body. (Lord Russel demonstrated taking the length of one's own body, and the Pins collapsed with laughter.) With that stick one went to the river. There one held the stick firmly in one's mouth and then began to sink into the water. This sinking must be done slowly and with patience; for as the tail and then the hinder portions went under, the fleas rushed north, up onto one's back. As that back descended in its turn, the fleas ran higher, ahead of the water lest they drown— sinister critters, they were, quite committed to their own lives! They huddled in the neck and behind the ears and on the crown of one's head. Now, when one had slid one's neck into the water as well, one must take a deep breath, hold it, and slowly lower one's whole head under water. The fleas, panicked and confused by the flood, would rush to the snout and, after that, leap onto the stick. Behold! One's body is totally underwater, and the fleas are totally on a stick. Spit out the stick and let it float away. Wait. Come up for air. Rejoice! It is done.

Ten Pin flashed a look at Five Pin, who flashed a look

at One Pin. Then Ten Pin fell down on the ground with a great shout and began to scratch his little body wherever the down grew yellow. Pins Five and One followed suit.

"Uncle! Uncle! It's getting worse," cried Ten Pin. "It was bad last night; but it's terrible today."

The Fox stood back, put his paws together, and looked on them with pity.

"Dear, dear," he said, reaching into their storm, attempting to help scratch, then snatching his paw back again. Quickly he took another tack: "Would you, Pin the Tenth," he shouted, "diagnose it as, *er*, irritation?"

"Terrible irritation, Uncle."

"As in, say, a *leaping* irritation?"

"Terrible leaping irritation of the skin!"

"Or, from another point of medical view, would you, perhaps, consider it a *galloping* irritation?"

"Oh, Uncle, it gallops and leaps and claws all over us!"

"Fleas?"

"Fleas! Yes, fleas! Oh, *such* fleas!"

"And you said terrible?" The Fox's eyes ran with sympathy. "I believe I heard you to mention terrible. And it is, after all, the first day of the summer."

With luminous honesty Ten Pin said: "This is the most terrible case of fleas that I have ever known."

"THEN TO THE NORTH!" cried the Fox, suddenly running furious circles around the Pins. "TENTH PIN, TO THE NORTH AND PICK YOU OUT A LIKELY STICK!"

Ten Pin scooted away without another question.

"WESTWARD, FIFTH PIN!" Lord Russel bellowed as he ran his tight, intense circles around the two remaining Pins. "SEEK YOUR STICK IN THE REGIONS OF THE WEST!"

Five Pin was gone.

"AND LET THE FIRST OF ALL PINS DO HIS SEARCHING IN THE EAST!"

One Pin zipped away to do so.

"WE'LL MEET AT THE RIVER! TAKE THE ROAD TO THE

RIVER!" For a moment the Fox flew after his own tail before he fully realized that he was alone. But as soon as that piece of information dawned on him, he fell into a sudden heap, thoroughly worn out from his excitement. By chance, his chin landed on his tail—welcome chance. Lord Russel fell asleep.

Beryl's fears were altogether lost on Chauntecleer; and his nasal efforts to calm her only made the fear bitter in her soul. When the respectful amount of time had been paid him, then, but without satisfaction, she lowered her head and left his presence. For just a few minutes she took herself to a hidden place, where she could pray earnestly on the Pins' behalf and where she could compose herself, so that the children would not see her afraid. After that, she went to gather them in.

But the circle, when she came to it, was empty.

"Oh, Lord," Beryl breathed, catching at her breast, "gone!"

Anger flashed into her eyes, that they hadn't listened to her. She bustled everywhere in the yard, scratched grass, where sometimes they hid, fidgeted into hollows, poked into all the corners of the Coop, always crying out their names. *They had left the circle!* And now she found them nowhere where they ought to be.

All propriety forgotten, she burst into the Coop to find Chauntecleer for the second time that day. But neither was he to be found. Beryl could not know that the Rooster had taken with him Pertelote and Mundo Cani to show them the southern flood—and the Coop was empty, of all save herself alone. There was no help for her from any corner. She couldn't even share the bad news.

Soon her anger melted into fear again; and fear turned into guilt.

"Why did I leave them alone?" she said aloud, shrugging her shoulders and turning in helpless little circles. "I

[117]

knew they shouldn't be alone. Children! They're no more than children! But Beryl left them alone."

Then, before the tears could come, Beryl did a thing which is, perhaps, never to be explained. Violently she grabbed a broom, and in a white fury she spent an hour cleaning the empty Coop all on her own—singing, at the top of her lungs. The floor, the walls, the roosts, the nests, and the very ceiling she made to dazzle with cleanliness; and every piece of goods and furniture she placed precisely in its proper place. Order! Lord, how her soul wanted order and cleanliness now; and the more she broke her back to get it, the better it was.

"Madam!" A cold, stentorian voice roared at her from the doorway. Beryl had to look twice to see Tick-tock the Black Ant standing there; and she had to think twice in order to cool her fury and to stop for him.

"Madam, you may wish to know that the children of your heart are loose in the forest. While you sing your songs here—heedless"—Tick-tock's voice was brittle, frozen, heavy with ice—"your charges, nurse, are bucking about the forest looking for sticks! They told my workers that they had plans to go to the river—"

"The river!" shrieked the Hen.

"—and obediently my workers reported to me." Having delivered his message, the Ant was about to turn on his heel. But a Hen overran him with such passion that he fell out of the doorway and bent his nose out of shape.

"A blind nurse is not a nurse," Beryl wept as she hurried out of the yard, southward to the river. "A fool is nothing but a fool. Alas, my heart, that ever I should wink and cease to care for them. I'll nevermore be nurse to the three little children. Oh, my Lord, I'm not worthy. I'm not worthy!"

It was some little time after this that Lord Russel the Fox bethought himself to rise and go, and to see about the

Chicks. It had been an enormously fine day for him. He had taken a particular pleasure in revealing to the Pins the trick about the fleas; and, on account of that, he had taken a particular pleasure in the nap which followed. It was a nap of the reputable, of one successful in his position, whose success has been noted and applauded by others. More than that, it had been a *dry* nap, so that the Fox had been reluctant to get up even after he had awakened. Therefore, Lord Russel stretched the pleasure of it and lay still before making his decision to go.

Then he arose and aimed himself south, toward the river, where he intended to see how well the Pins had learned their lesson.

Since Foxes travel faster than Chicks, he made no great hurry of his going. Rather, he made mental notes of how the dry twigs crackled underneath his step. Casually he glanced about to find a good stick of his own. And several times over he took his own measure, just to be sure of the stick he found.

The forest knew a fine, dry breeze; in its high places, the soil itself was dry: a good day! And on the way to the river Lord Russel once in a while scrubbed his paws with the oil of the rue plant. This was another trick of his, and one which he planned to deliver to the Pins tomorrow: It threw anyone who might be pursuing him off his scent.

Suddenly, from the top of a hill, the Fox saw Chauntecleer and his company as they were returning to the Coop. They moved slowly, obviously talking with one another as they went. Lord Russel judged that their talk was grave and important, for so their slow steps seemed to indicate. But he couldn't hear it from his distance.

He was just about to raise his stick and to halloo them, cheered to have come upon them so unexpectedly. But something caught his attention instead—a small pile of white and yellow in the path ahead of Chauntecleer. With foreboding, the Fox squinted to see clearly what

[119]

it was. He wanted, and he did not want, to know. He blinked several times, his poor heart racing. Then his eyes focused, and he was struck dumb.

He saw a Hen and three Chicks, lying down together.

Unable to speak a word, Lord Russel glanced back at the company walking down the path. Pertelote was saying something, while Chauntecleer shook his head. Chauntecleer put his wings apart in a gesture of helplessness, and then he began to speak while the other two listened. He spoke strongly, sweeping his wings wide, as if he were referring to all of his land. Always, the three continued to walk closer to the soft heap, while Lord Russel, fixed in his silence, could do nothing but watch.

Suddenly Mundo Cani stopped, went rigid, and stared straight ahead of him. Chauntecleer looked at the Dog; then he, too, looked straight ahead. The Rooster froze stiff. He stood absolutely still for a moment. Then he spoke a word to the other two without looking at them and walked forward by himself.

Lord Russel felt boulders in his throat. He couldn't cry warnings. He couldn't whisper. He could only watch.

The Rooster came to the place where the Hen and the Chicks were lying. He reached to touch them once. And then he stood wooden for a very long time.

A strange sound filled the air. Lord Russel heard it. It was a keening wail, as if the wind were passing away through the branches of naked trees. But now there was no wind.

Where she stood, Pertelote had turned away from the sight in front of her. She was looking back toward the river. Her head was high. She was weeping for her children.

The sound of her weeping loosened the Fox from his sorrowful trance. He began to run, though he knew that Chauntecleer watched him as he came. When he drew near, Lord Russel saw that it was Beryl who lay beside the children.

"I was going to—to meet them there," the Fox said miserably.

"Where?" Chauntecleer spoke quietly. The Fox could not look at him.

"At the, *ah*. Beside, *ah*, the— They were to have, *ah*, brought—"

"Where?" the Rooster said again.

"—sticks. The river."

"The river," Chauntecleer breathed. A low, menacing growl began in Mundo Cani's chest; his head was slung low between his powerful shoulder blades, his eyes smoking. Lord Russel cringed.

"Shut up," the Rooster said, and the Dog was quiet.

"They are dead, Lord Russel," Chauntecleer said quietly. "Sticks and rivers, floods and thunderclouds, serpents aground or flying—my children are dead, Lord Russel."

"I know," the Fox said, and he said no more.

"And the sadness is—they were killed."

Beryl lay on her back, as if she had been struck across her throat, a frightful blow. Her head was loose and turned to the side, because her neck was broken. Ten Pin, Five Pin, and One Pin were lying in a little group beside her. Their backs were together as if they were merely leaning that way for the comfort. But their beaks were open, their eyes closed, and their chests each bore the marks of a bite. A circle had been marked in the ground around all four.

"Now we will carry them back to the Coop," Chauntecleer said. Mundo Cani came forward.

"Lord Russel will bear the nurse, Beryl," said Chauntecleer, and suddenly the Dog did not know what to do. "Tenderly, Russel. You shall walk most tenderly with this lady."

Chauntecleer watched him narrowly to see whether his walk was indeed a tender one.

Lord Russel was suffering mightily. He had not yet

[121]

looked at the Rooster. Nevertheless, he lifted Beryl in his jaws and began to walk back to the Coop alone. He walked tenderly. And he was grateful for Chauntecleer's remembrance of him.

Then Chauntecleer spread his wings and gathered his children together beneath them. He raised his head and held his children to his breast.

"Mundo Cani Dog." His voice was as thin as a reed. "Please look after the Beautiful Pertelote, and bring her."

[sixteen] *Chauntecleer's prayer is met by one thing, John Wesley's rage by another*

o anyone who might have seen him standing on the Coop that night, Chauntecleer would have seemed to be black iron. A breeze tugged at his feathers; they flipped forward on his back—ragged, vagrant. But the Rooster himself was iron and immoveable. On this night he had nothing to do with breezes.

At dusk he had crowed the crow of grief. But there had been no satisfaction in it. He had done it more the Lord of the land than father of the children: abruptly, briefly, bitterly, formally—a bitten crow. And all who lay awake listening were left more agonized than had the crow rung truly with Chauntecleer's deeper sadness.

But then, when the crow was done, the Rooster was not done. And so he held his position for hours against the night, while the animals beneath him, though they did not sleep, honored him with stillness and silence.

"You, God," Chauntecleer finally said; but his iron body did not move. His muscles were taut wire. Had someone touched him at that moment, he would have spun and murdered him.

"You, God, promise—then break promises," he said. "You give. You warm me to your gift. You cause love to go out of me to your gift—and then you kill me. You kill my gift.

"I did not want this land. I would just as soon have traveled my way, taken what came to me by chance and left the rest. I would just as soon have gone a-mucking through this world of yours unnoticed, untouched by—

your—righteous—hand. Then I may have been empty, but not bereft; I didn't know what blessing you had it in you to offer. Then I may have been alone, but not lonely; I didn't know what love you could ordain. You, God! You took me out of my life! You set me into this false place. You made me believe in you. You gave me hope! O my God, you taught me to *hope*! And then you killed me."

Chauntecleer trembled where he stood. He closed his eyes against the darkness to control the trembling—not because he thought his words were wicked; simply because he did not want to tremble before God.

"If I had never had sons, how could I lose sons? If I had never ruled a land, how could I fear to lose the land? It is in the *giving* that treachery begins. If I had never loved these animals, which the almighty God put into my keeping, I would not die thinking that they may die.

"But by *your* will I am where I am. By *your* will things are what they are. Now by *my* will I demand to hear it from your own mouth: *Where are my sons?* Why is Pertelote weeping underneath me in the Coop? And what am I to say to her? Bear them, bless them, watch them; then ball them into tiny balls and stuff them in the earth! I'll tell her. She'll be comforted. I'll tell her of the will of God."

Chauntecleer drove hot air deep into his lungs. He roared: "And by *my* will I demand to know now—it is most certainly time now to know: *O God, where are you?* Why have you hidden your face from us? Why now, of all times, when things are on the rim of disaster, have you turned away? Nine months! I have not seen the stars for nine months! In nine months we have not seen a single passing of the sun, and the moon is only a memory. Faith, right? By faith I should believe that the spheres still turn above these everlasting clouds. Tell me! Tell me! Infinite God, tell me what we have done to be shut from the rest of the universe! But you won't tell me. You've dropped us in a bucket and let us be. It wears a person out, you know. Yeah, well."

[124]

Then the Rooster did move. His head sank between his shoulders. His wings drooped. He broke into tears. "My sons, my sons," he wept. "Why didn't God let me die instead of you?"

Chauntecleer sobbed several moments together. Then he spoke in another voice, without raising his head.

"Aye. He wills that I work his work in this place. Indeed. I am left behind to labor. Right.

"And one day he may show his face beneath his damnable clouds to tell me what that work might be; what's worth so many tears; what's so important in his sight that it needs to be done *this* way. . . .

"O my sons!" Chauntecleer suddenly wailed at the top of his lungs, a light flaring before it goes out: *"How much I want you with me!"*

The dark land everywhere held still, as if on purpose before such a ringing, echoing cry. The dark sky said nothing. The Rooster, with not an effort to save himself, sagged, rolled down the roof, slipped over the edge of the Coop, and fell heavily to the ground. Wind and sobs together were knocked out of him; he lay dazed.

And then it was that the Dun Cow came to him.

She put her soft nose against him, to nudge him into a more peaceful position. Gently she arranged his head so that he might clearly see her. Her sweet breath went into his nostrils, and he assumed that he woke up; but he didn't move. The Dun Cow took a single step back from the Rooster, then, and looked at him.

Horns strangely dangerous on one so soft stood wide away and sharp from either side of her head.

Her eyes were liquid with compassion—deep, deep, as the earth is deep. Her brow knew his suffering and knew, besides that, worlds more. But the goodness was that, though this wide brow knew so much, yet it bent over his pain alone and creased with it.

Chauntecleer watched his own desolation appear in the brown eyes of the Cow, then sink so deeply into them that

[125]

she shuddered. Her eyes pooled as she looked at him. The tears rose and spilled over. And then she was weeping even as he had wept a few minutes ago—except without the anger. Strangely, Chauntecleer felt an urge to comfort *her*; but at this moment he was no Lord, and the initiative was not in him. A simple creature only, he watched— felt—the miracle take place. Nothing changed: The clouds would not be removed, nor his sons returned, nor his knowledge plenished. But there was this. His grief had become her grief, his sorrow her own. And though he grieved not one bit less for that, yet his heart made room for her, for her will and wisdom, and he bore the sorrow better.

The Dun Cow lay down next to the Rooster and spent the rest of the night with him. She never spoke a word, and Chauntecleer did not sleep. But for a little while they were together.

At dawn Chauntecleer crowed lauds; and then he went alone into his Coop.

There was movement there in the dim light, as if the animals were waking up. But that movement was all pretending, since not one of them had been asleep. No rain, no wind—but there had been a storm that night nonetheless; and the silence of the last several hours had been unreadable. So the animals had blinked and breathed their ways through the long night, all of them awake: the Hens, the Mice, the Fox, the Dog, the Black Ant, too; the beautiful and mourning Pertelote—and a Weasel.

Everyone saw solemnity in their Lord. Everyone permitted him to walk to his perch undisturbed. Everyone except—

"Rooster knows who, don't he?" said John Wesley Weasel from a position directly in front of Chauntecleer.

But Chauntecleer hardly saw him. "I'm tired, John Wesley." His eyes rested instead on Pertelote; and by the bowing of her head he saw that she was filled with sorrow. She was also very tired and should sleep.

"John knows who!" snapped the Weasel. "Once is, always is! No changing the wicked. No teaching the vile!"

"Ah, John—speak to me at prime. Explain yourself then."

But the Weasel wouldn't let the Rooster pass.

"Is only clawing and killing for his like. Execution! Execution! Chop away his head!" He was warming to his subject.

Chauntecleer looked him in the eye for just a second, then looked away again. "You make no sense," he said. Compulsively he glanced back to Pertelote. She was shivering. The Rooster felt that the Weasel's chatter added trouble to her sorrow. "Clear out!" he commanded.

But John Wesley suddenly hunched his back so high that his fore and hind legs pressed against each other. It was a fighting posture. He had waited all the night long to say what burned inside of him, and now it swept him away:

"Hate him! Hate him!" he hissed, flashing his teeth. "One murders Chicks! One breaks a Hen what should live! Oh, how John does hate him!"

That triggered Mundo Cani. Reading threat, the Dog reared from his place at the door and plunged toward the Weasel to pitch him out.

"Off, mountain back!" cried the Weasel. "Touch me and I touch you with what for!" The Weasel's teeth were razor sharp and furious. His courage was phenomenal.

"Mundo Cani!" Chauntecleer ordered. "Sit down!" He did. "You, John Wesley." He glared at the Weasel. "I don't ever want to hear that again. Never again in this Coop or on this land do I want to hear that you hate a living soul."

"One wants hating," the Weasel persisted. "Pleads for hating. Kills for hating."

"Not hating, John Wesley."

"Look what he—"

"Not hating!" Chauntecleer's crow was full of thunder. Hens tottered and began walking on their roosts. The Weasel cowered. But yet he didn't stop talking.

"Here's one Double-u," he mumbled, "what won't kiss no Rat."

Then Chauntecleer gazed at him with sudden understanding. "Wise little Weasel. So you think you know who killed my children."

"Think! I think and then I know. I *know!*"

"Good thinking, perhaps, John Wesley. But your conclusions are bad. He couldn't have done it."

"Was Nezer," said the Weasel—and that did it.

Immediately the Coop blew up: confusion, motion, wild clucking. Jacinth streaked through the air with no place to land, beating her wings as if she were cursed. The others responded, leaping in place and turning circles.

John Wesley was pleased. They, at least, believed him. "Ebenezer Rat!" he cried above the blizzard.

Chauntecleer crowed for order. He crowed again. He crowed a third time. But the Hens were letting loose the strain of a wakeful night. Yesterday's horror, last night's dumb waiting, suddenly had a name, and that name had broken their control.

Chauntecleer moved. He laid a wing on Jacinth and another on Topaz and held them close until they were still. He did this to one after another until they all knew him by his touch and had finally settled into an uneasy peace.

"Did none of you sleep last night?" he asked.

They only looked at him, and he was moved to pity them.

"God help us all," he said.

Then, while things were momentarily balanced, he rose to a perch above them. "All right. Take some comfort in this," he said, "that it couldn't have been Ebenezer Rat. Whatever Nezer is, whatever he might wish to do, he couldn't have broken Beryl's neck as it was broken. Ebenezer can break egg shells, and he is wicked enough to eat the eggs in them. But this is just a fact: If he went against a full-grown Hen, either he would lose to her, or else her death would have been much bloodier than Beryl's."

"Nezer has a grudge." The Weasel pressed his argument in spite of the Rooster's words.

Chauntecleer whirled on him: "And a grudge may be strong. But a grudge isn't strength!" Right now he despised arguing with the insolent Weasel; but he desperately didn't want his Hens aroused again.

"Can want revenge, ha! Little grows big for revenge. Puny gets strong for revenge. Then hunt him! Kill him!"

"John Wesley Weasel, look at yourself! *Those* are the words of revenge!"

"Who kills three Chicks? Who leaves none to be prince? Who chooses three to kill three? Him what was humbled by their father: Nezer Rat!"

"John, don't you see what you're doing? Now you want me to choose one to kill one. You want me to do what he did. I should become a rat to kill a Rat! Avenge revenge? Why, that's sin—and a poor, defeating sin at that!"

"No. Not."

"What then? Why do you push it so?"

"Let John Double-u be Double-u. John hunts him. John kills him"—the Weasel threw back his head, unmistakable contempt for Chauntecleer in his eyes—"for you."

"Proof!" said the Rooster. "I want—"

Suddenly a high, tiny voice pierced the air: *"Out! Out! Out!"* The voice came from underneath the floor, bleating, chopped with panic. A windless skittering under the floorboard silenced both Rooster and Weasel; then the Wee Widow Mouse shot from her hole.

[129]

"Get him out of there!" she beseeched Chauntecleer, backing away even from him. "Please tell him to go away!"

The Hens began a nervous jerking. The Rooster hardly knew what to ask.

"He wants in the back hole," the Widow pleaded. "Please tell him to go away." The young Mice were tumbling out after her, bewildered.

Without a word Chauntecleer flew from his perch, directly out of the Coop. He spun round the corner to the back.

There—half in, half out of the Widow's back hole—he saw a body. The head had gone in first, and then the rest of the body could get no further. Yet, weakly, the four legs were pushing forward with a hopeless will. But the entrance was impossible. Two strong, white feathers were buried in the back of this body, their span much too wide to let it pass; so it was against these feathers that the legs were pushing, and the feathers denied it entrance.

Chauntecleer heard Mundo Cani speak behind him: "Ebenezer Rat," the Dog said.

"Just so," said the Rooster quietly. "Pull him out, Mundo Cani."

The Dog took the body between his two paws and drew it backward.

Even on the open ground Nezer continued to tread his legs, ignorant that his home was no longer in front of him. His eyes were closed. He was nearly dead. He had an impossibly deep wound on the side of his neck. His fur was matted with blood.

John Wesley Weasel stood beside them. "You see?" he said.

"I see, you impertinent fool!" Chauntecleer hissed without lifting his eyes from the dying Rat. "Now, Weasel, *you* look and see!"

He turned Ebenezer's head to the side. The wound yawned. But the lesson was elsewhere: Clamped in the

Rat's mouth was a foul section of a serpent, chewed away from its greater body. Organs enough clung shredded and gouty to the flesh to prove that that one had died as well. It must have been a hideous fight.

"Talk, Weasel," Chauntecleer hissed, "when you know in God's name what you are talking about."

In all his life Chauntecleer had never known Ebenezer Rat to speak a single word. Therefore he didn't expect an explanation now, and he asked no questions. He said, "Peace, Nezer," and he watched in silence until the legs stopped their treading and the body relaxed. The feathers lolled a little; and then they were perfectly still.

Ebenezer Rat was dead.

Chauntecleer took the serpent from the Rat's mouth. Then he yanked both feathers from their sockets and threw them violently at the wind. He stroked Ebenezer's fur smooth, groaning while he did. He kissed the Rat.

And then he leaped high—to the top of the Coop.

"I want a Council!" he cried; his voice echoed from the forest in the morning air: "Council!"

"Every one of you! Have your kin here by the afternoon. Present your breed before me! Let not one of them stay away, not women, not children, not the old—everyone! Have them *all* here by the afternoon!"

Though none of them had slept, they all took to their heels and left—John Wesley Weasel among them; and the dawn light saw them disappear.

"Where is Scarce?" cried the Rooster. "Scarce, where are you?"

"Here," said a small, buzzing voice. "Never, never gone."

Chauntecleer looked and saw him just off the end of his beak. It did take some looking to see Scarce, even when one knew where he was. Scarce was a Mosquito. Scarce was all Mosquitoes; but then, all Mosquitoes are one. So they were all known by the one name, Scarce. And if someone had spoken to one of them, he had spoken to them all. And if someone avoided all of them, yet there was always one he couldn't avoid. On the whole, there was no better messenger than Scarce.

"I want you to put it into every ear in my land," Chauntecleer said, "that I will have a Council in the afternoon. Do more than inform them. And more than urge them, *command* them to come. No one—no matter how large and powerful, how small and cunning—is safe who stays away. Perilous times, Scarce. I want every creature at this place by the afternoon."

Scarce simply disappeared, and his buzzing went with him.

Then Chauntecleer went inside a hollow Coop to be with Pertelote. He went wordless, and wordless he sat beside her. He knew the size of her sorrow.

[SEVENTEEN] Comings

Between yesterday and today, between the time of her wretched discovery and the moment she fell into an exhausted sleep, between death and death, Pertelote had said nothing; and none, not even Chauntecleer, knew for sure what went through her mind. One thing, however, she did say.

Chauntecleer had been sitting beside her for an hour—not touching her, nor even looking at her, but yet writhing in his soul on her account—when she shifted position ever so slightly. Immediately his senses quivered, alert.

She said, "Beryl was a good nurse."

Chauntecleer nearly made a noise of agreement, nearly sought to start conversation. But he thought better of it.

"This sacrifice was not meant for her," Pertelote said. And then that was all.

An hour later the Rooster concluded by her breathing that she had fallen asleep, and he was relieved. Strangely, her sleep set him somewhat free. Since he himself had no trouble talking—indeed, lived, moved, experienced, and identified experience by the words of his mouth—her silence was a suffocation for him and her distance a torment. They bound him. They damned his love to helplessness. They made him feel mortal and small next to such self-possession. If she would offer him words, then he could heal her with words. Moreover, then he would win the right to spill his own feelings into the open by words—and could do so with impunity and without the fear that he might diminish himself by the blather. But when she slept, words were not even a remote consideration. And the

[133]

sleep itself was a kind of unspoken word, signifying trust. Therefore Chauntecleer often waited for his Pertelote to fall asleep first before he let himself—a tiny, private conquest; a bitty proof of his own self-possession. And therefore her sleep on this particular afternoon set him free.

The Rooster, without leaving Pertelote's side, turned his attention to the other Hens asleep in the Coop. Despite the daylight, he had commanded it; so they slept. But he heard the nervous cries of their dreams. He saw them shudder, rise up on their legs without waking. He knew that—though the name alarmed them—they had wished that the enemy *had* been Ebenezer Rat, because they knew him. Nezer had a head and tail which could be measured, a track which could be recognized, a wickedness which could be laid low, a name! He was a Rat, an animal: He was one of them. Feared, invidious, criminal, and right worthy the punishment he received—yet one of them, for all of that. But *now* the Hens dreamed faceless dreams, fought the bodyless, the eyeless—gibbering, screeching, wordless, nameless, immeasurable, unutterable, the enemy was in their dreams hagging them. And these dreams were the worse because sleep in the afternoon is a heated, sweaty, fretful affair. But the Rooster had commanded it.

Chauntecleer watched his Hens and his stricken wife with yearning.

Middle afternoon. Lord Russel, the Fox of Good Sense, stepped out of the forest, a solitary figure. He glanced furtively around the empty Coop yard, then snatched himself back into the brush. For the space of ten minutes the yard stood abandoned, flat, and still. Then another Fox, not Russel, twitched into view and slunk from bush to bush. One by one Russel's kin began to creep into the yard, obviously uncomfortable to be in open spaces, but coming. Cousins, male and female; red coats and black tips to their tails, as if the tails had been dipped in ink; silently on padded feet, and singly they came. They were a breed all unused to talking with one another; so it had gone against Russel's nature to gather them together, but he had nonetheless done it, and they came: Nieces and nephews, second and third cousins, aunts and uncles unto the fourth and fifth generation, the Foxes came.

Then the ground began to move, and the astonished Foxes rushed together for safety. Their eyeballs popped. The whole yard slid, shifted, crumbled toward the Coop—until Lord Russel himself, the most ecumenical among his relatives, began to giggle. It wasn't the ground moving at all, but countless thousands of Ants, like living dust upon the earth, come to the Council. Black Ants marching. Red Ants, fiery Red Ants full of the vicious bite. Hill builders and ground diggers, some as large as a Fox's tooth, some as small as grass seed, tickering and traveling in such masses that they could be heard—or else the earth itself was whispering. Like flowing sand they closed upon the Coop.

The Foxes had come from the north. The Ants, like thought, had come from anywhere. Now, out of the east and wet with the sticky water of the Liver-brook, Otters tumbled into the yard, scooting chaos into the Antian dignity which had preceded them, snapping left and right like a hundred fish, altogether unrestrained by the gravity of the Council, playing games. So abashed had John Wesley been by his morning mistake that he had swallowed his pride and carried the Rooster's command even to the Mad House of Otter—relatives of his which he would otherwise have disavowed with a curse and a quarrel.

If John had relatives which he classed below himself, he also had relatives who classed themselves above him. Had he swallowed some pride approaching the Mad House of Otter? Well, verily, then he gagged on pride approaching

[135]

the Family Mink. But they came, too. Disdainfully they came, carrying their own approved food (enough for a day's excursion, a sad miscalculation!), their little heads and their bright beady eyes high and distant. They were appalled at the presence of so many Ants; and as for the Otters—on that matter they wouldn't even deliver an opinion.

And the Weasels themselves appeared, stumbling curiously in the light. Their eyes had been made for the night. Only John Wesley Weasel among them had learned adjustment. But Chauntecleer had called a Council for the afternoon, and they were here.

A deep, menacing buzz—at exactly the height of the treetops—announced the Bees; and they descended.

Rabbits blew out of the forest like cottonwood before a high wind: thumpers, jacks, stringy grey and puffy white; some lop-eared and some with ears like nickels, every ear twitching in every direction to judge the mood of the place.

The Deer walked out in grace.

Sparrows flocked, then settled, unnaturally, upon the ground.

The Pigs lumbered in, breathing heavily,

The Ducks, the Geese, and the Swans took note of one another in various nasal languages (they were a loose-knit family; but they *were* a family nonetheless, and it was proper for families to take note of one another) and squatted in separate areas around the Coop.

Sheep tiptoed in, and wished nervously that Chauntecleer would hurry up and appear.

Then the easy sequence of the coming was broken. The nice distinctions among families, which had heretofore been maintained, were absolutely shattered.

For now the whole forest raised a careless, stupid noise—a guttural, pleasant, throaty, meaningless chatter so foreign to its regular nobility. Stuttered words tumbled from between the trees, like: "Goo-goo-good!" Inane noises like: "Ge-ge-get a gallop on, my bubble-brother! We're tardy-dee-dee!" Then a hundred voices chorused together: "Goda-goda-speed the rutabaga Rooster! And goo-goo-good afternoon to him!" And a thousand said: "Galoot!" for no perceptible reason whatever. All of these sounds—constituted chiefly of bumps, burps, and g's—thumped out of the forest. And then, from the wooded uplands of Chauntecleer's land, where they did not even know enough to come in out of the rain, but where they learned good breeding and decorum in abundance, here came the Wild Turkeys. Ridiculous heads on ridiculous, tubby bodies with ridiculous, good-natured chatter in their throats, they came. Smiling, nodding, and burping on everyone, from the Ant to the Deer, no matter. Greeting this one and that, they spread out among the company in the yard. Salutations, compliments, well wishes, they sprinkled on every available head as if it were their business—and, indeed, they were convinced that it was: *Someone*, so their reasoning, must cast a little cheer wherever he goes. There's little enough of that in the world.

The animals came. Not representatives only—*all* the animals who dwelled in Chauntecleer's land.

Animals brown and soft, animals quick and grey, animals ruddy, animals black and melancholy, animals with piercing, suspicious eyes, animals plumed and animals pelted, winged animals and those footed for the ground, the fleet and the contemplative, the leapers and the dodgers and the crawlers and the carriers, the racers and the trotters and the climbers and the fallers, singers, croakers, whistlers, barkers, gabblers, philosophers, orators, and mute—they all pressed into the great yard around Chauntecleer's Coop; they had heard the word which Scarce had borne to them; they had obeyed.

And having come, what a sight they made! What a jumbled, whichaway, particolored traffic they made as they

[137]

moiled around finding places for themselves. Heads and ears, noses and eyes, backs of every stripe and pattern— a very carpet of animals. The rest of the land was deserted; but this place boiled with life—obedient and waiting.

It was wonderful that in all this rabbled congregation, no one stepped on another one's tail. Perhaps there was a reason for that. For it was noticeable, too, that these were every one of them the meek of the earth. They were meek by inheritance. Only John Wesley and his kin were born to meanness; but Chauntecleer had some time ago made them meek by instruction. They were catechized into meekness.

And as he took his position now atop the Coop, Chauntecleer wondered painfully if he should ever have done such a thing, taken blood out of the Weasels' eyes. For what were these before him? As many as they were, as noisy and as varied as they were, what were these against the evil which now assailed them? Chauntecleer looked out over this enormous company of souls, and he was silent for a time.

One by one, family by family, he recognized all his animals, and his heart rushed out to them. Who was he to command them? A nothing! He was himself weak and filled with fault. He was afraid, as Pertelote knew right well. He was ignorant and foolish.

Yet, what an enemy he must lead them against!

And dear God! Where were their claws with which to fight a fight? Where were the teeth for ripping and tearing? Where among this assembly was the heart to kill an enemy? Look at them! They hadn't the least idea even of the purpose of this Council. They came only at a command. Then how in God's name would they battle? Fight? War? *Win* a bloody war? How can the meek of the earth save themselves against the damnable evil which feeds on them?

All of these things Chauntecleer thought in a tiny space

[138]

of time. All of this burned through his mind while the noise and the contumely died down and the animals composed themselves to hear him speak.

And then, in a flash before he crowed a greeting, he noticed Mundo Cani far in the rear of the congregation. The Dog had brought no family. He must have none, thought the Rooster.

But the Dog did have a companion; and the moment Chauntecleer recognized her, two separate feelings buzzed his brains: both gratitude and resentment. She was the Dun Cow; her presence stilled the Rooster's soul. But she was talking—talking low, insistently, into Mundo Cani's ear, who himself kept his head bowed; and she was not looking at Chauntecleer. In spite of the gravity of the moment; in spite of the importance of his high position and the office which must now demand his whole attention, Chauntecleer was piqued: The Dun Cow hadn't spoken to him so much as a single word. What was this attraction to a Dog with a bulbous nose?

But almost before he commanded them, his beak opened and his throat crowed a crow of salute to the thousands of animals in front of him.

[EIGHTEEN] *The Council has a sting in its tail*

ow old are we?" Chauntecleer cried, throwing the crow from deep in his chest. It would be some time before he was through, and he didn't want his voice finally to break at any point in his speaking to the assembly. His figure as well as his words, he knew, carried the message. A faltering figure would weaken the message and unsettle the animals. *Two* messages, really. He must encourage their faith. That first. Without that they would wither before the second message and die helpless before the enemy. And the second message would be to tell them that there *was* an enemy. Chauntecleer suffered at that thought. He truly did not know how he was going to tell them. He lacked words.

"How many years have we lived in this land? How many years has the land been good to us, feeding our children and keeping us alive?

"Ho, the ancient among you! Count the years and number the generations. We are very old in the land.

"Ho, the mothers among you! Tell me of your children. Do they know how to laugh? Do they run in the daylight, and is the sound of their laughter sweet to you? Do they know how to sleep in contentment? Tell me of your children, mothers! When last did you stand at their beds and weep because they died for want of food? When did *you* die inside, seeing them sent away to fight in the wars? No, I will tell you. Never! Their laughter and their rest, their fullness and their peace, have been everlasting in this land. The land, and the time, and the children—these are the Lord's doing!

"Then let the creatures of the Lord say Amen!"

In a thousand separate ways, the animals around the Coop lifted up their voices. They said, "Amen!" They had begun to listen. Good! Chauntecleer had found his rhythm, and the Council had begun. Good, good.

"Ho, the fathers among you! Tell me about your peace. When did you look for food, and it was not there? When, in the summer, did you seek out shade for your family, and there was none? When, in the winter, did you look to build a warm burrow and find neither the place nor the stuff for building? When, in all this age, did you ever begin a plan in joy, then find in sorrow that you could not finish it? Tell me, fathers, of your peace! For these are the things of frustration and despair—and in this land you have never known either one! Food, shade, warmth, and the divine ability to finish what you have begun, these the land has provided, and the land has provided so that you might provide! The Lord has permitted you to be what you were born to be. Then bless the Lord—

"And let the creatures of the Lord say Amen!"

"Amen! Amen!" The animals roared and thundered. "Amen!" They rose up and stood on their feet.

"Listen to me!" Chauntecleer cried from the roof of his Coop. His voice was hard and brilliant, like urgent lightning going out of his mouth. "Sit down and listen!"

He paused. They sat down again. He shot a glance to the Dun Cow. Then he closed his eyes and began to speak as if he were alone. But he could be heard. He told them a story.

"There was once a young Rooster born of hot and dry," he said, "a choleric, snappish, belligerent youth. He was raised by a gentle, tired, widowed mother in a land far south of this one. And this was long ago.

"A Wolf roamed that land, terrorizing the animals so badly that they shunned one another. They lived in suspicion. By betrayal they dealt with one another. But the young Rooster was unconcerned—because the havoc in the land gave him good pickings. He stole food from deserted homes and treasures from hasty hiding places, took daughters when it pleased him, and turned everyone else's evil to his advantage. He was equal to the ugliness of the world. And it was, in fact, a wretched, ugly world.

"But then the Wolf moved into the home of this Rooster's mother, demanding that she feed him and take care of him; and the Rooster was forced to watch while his mother brought meat to the Wolf's table, was forced to listen to the Wolf's heavy snoring.

"Now this was something different, and the Rooster was enraged.

" 'Fight him!' he demanded of his mother when the two were alone.

" 'I can't,' said his mother.

" 'You don't want to!' sneered the Rooster. And hard though this was on her, it was the truth.

" 'It is the will of the Lord,' she said more than once, and she refused nothing that the Wolf demanded of her. Neither would she join her son when he cursed the beast, but instead she warned her *son* against displeasing *God.* 'It is the will of the Lord,' she said often, gently.

"So the Rooster hated the Wolf and despised her Lord, both. If she would not, and if God could not, then he would himself fight the Wolf.

"He owned two iron spurs, weapons of his father: Gaff, they were named, and the Slasher. These he strapped to his legs one night, when the Wolf was sleeping. He wanted to wake his mother and send her away, but he couldn't without warning the Wolf. Suddenly, then, in the middle of the night, he leaped upon the beast, driving a spur into either side of his chest. The Wolf thrashed violently, but the Rooster rode him, screaming curses all the while and thrusting his spurs ever deeper. In his violence, the Wolf killed the mother; and then the Rooster killed the Wolf.

" 'The Lord's will,' thought the Rooster as he looked at

his poor mother; then he laughed at the Lord.

"He laughed even louder when the animals of that land condemned him for his own mother's death and banished him. He was not at all surprised by their cheap justice: for the world was a wretched, ugly place.

"But the young Rooster would avenge himself on them. He never removed Gaff and the Slasher. Instead he planned to kill the leaders of the land one at a time.

"But during the night, while the Rooster waited in a tree, the Lord appeared to him. The light was so bright that the Rooster fell out of his tree, stunned, full of terror.

" 'Get away from me,' the Rooster cried, 'or I'll die!' In the blinding light he saw himself, and he was a filthy piece of thing. One moment more under such a brilliance and he would be gone altogether. Worse, it seemed to him that the Lord could not but want to snuff so contemptible a life from the earth.

" 'Why do you hurt my creatures?' said the Lord out of his radiance.

" 'Your creatures!' moaned the Rooster.

" 'Why do you hurt me?' The light was a blaze. The young Rooster felt his heart afire. He answered nothing. He waited to die.

" 'Get up,' said the Lord. 'In the north you will find a land in need of a leader. I will give the land to you.'

" 'I can't,' said the Rooster. 'I'm nothing.'

" 'It is my will that you go,' said the Lord.

" 'But I am the least of all your creatures,' said the Rooster.

" 'You are mine,' said the Lord. 'Go!' So mighty, so glorious was the force of that final command that the Rooster both died and got up at once.

"When he came, he found the northern land in sad shambles. But by the power and the will of the same Lord—for the Rooster still was nothing—he saw peace made in this place. Craven animals came together and

[143]

became strong. Aimless lives, and days without purpose, began to smile and to work and to live with resolution. Order came to this land, because the Lord was worshiped and welcomed daily, seven times a day, by seven crows which the same Lord taught his Rooster. And as evidence of the Lord's labor here, the bandit Weasels, who once had lived for their own sakes only, turned and began to live for others. Not the Rooster—the Lord did this thing: And the animals produced; and the land provided. . . .

"By the Lord was a Rooster transfigured!

"By the Lord was a land made good!"

Chauntecleer's eyes were open again. Again he was standing full figure on the top of the Coop, sweeping his gaze all across the animals around him, while the animals sat in wonderment.

"Some of you know this from your own experience; but none of you has known it so well as you do now. That's why I tell you my story: I am a witness! The Lord loves you with an abiding love. He will not leave you desolate—or else why did I come to you out of the south *by his will*?"

A rumbling rolled through the congregation. Chauntecleer's story was like a rock dropped into a lake: It took time for the swallowing and for the waves to settle into knowledge. Chauntecleer gave them that time and stared away at the Dun Cow while he did. Now she was looking at him. Now her eyes shone like suns, and he was greatly relieved: Someone here knew the effort it took to tell that story. But in the daylight he noticed, again, how lethal her long horns looked.

As the rumbling began to die—but before the yard was quiet—Chauntecleer seized the wonder of the congregation and drove it in his own directions, crying in a loud voice:

"Now that time is come which one day *had* to come. God breathed faith into us so that *today* we might be faithful. For generations God won trust from us so that *today* we might trust him. Years and years of providence had this purpose: that for one day we might not faint, but believe in him—and fight—stouthearted, fight—and win—and live!

"O my beloved: but the odds are terrible!" Chauntecleer said in another voice. "And therefore I called the Council."

Fight? New rumblings passed over the congregation. Heads bobbed and turned to one another. Only the members of the Coop held still, as if transfixed, because, though they knew little, they knew more than these others. *Fight?* Whenever before have we had to fight? Why *fight?*

"The Beautiful Pertelote," Chauntecleer said quietly, as if he were finishing the story which he had started before—and the assembly instantly hushed, straining to hear his words. "The Beautiful Pertelote was a mother like you, once."

Was?

"Her children ran and laughed in the daylight, slept with contentment, ate and were healthy."

Were?

"I was a father. I provided for my family. I knew peace. To every one of their questions I had an answer. Every one of my plans had a good ending—"

Why does he say "had"? Why does he speak in "was"?

"But now Pertelote weeps beside three empty beds. And I have learned that the best of plans can die before they are done. My children are dead."

Dead! The entire congregation froze at the word.

Now Chauntecleer had to speak very fast, but very clearly—before the calm exploded:

"If the murderer were from among us, I would not tell you of the murder. It wouldn't concern you. But he's from another place, another land. And the death of my children is only his first word to us—to us all. This is the day which had to come. The enemy is frightful and full of power and

[145]

hateful and of a mind to murder all the children, to ruin all the land, to slaughter this place with the next, to leave no soul alive. We've got to be one as we have been one! For he is many. We've got to prepare! We will have to fight him when he comes. But we can! In the name of God we can—and by God triumph!"

But it so often happens that first words steal from the last words; and at this particular moment, the animals were stunned rather than encouraged. "Murder," "enemy" rang in their ears. "Triumph" they hadn't heard at all. And the explosion which Chauntecleer expected—that never came.

For so many animals to be in one place, the silence was astonishing. Here, there, and yonder back to the forest, the eyes stared at Chauntecleer as if there were so much more to be said. He had opened them up. Now they wanted filling—and suddenly the Rooster was lost, exhausted. Mouths drooped open, because every creature had forgotten himself. Ears stood up, twitching, reaching for a sound, some other sound besides the lonely note of peril. And Chauntecleer didn't know what else to put in those ears. Had they heard nothing of his first important message? What did they think—that he was just dithering when he spoke of God's faithfulness to them? So much preparation for this moment, and their ears had been stone!

Chauntecleer's stomach hurt as if he had been kicked there. He had said it all, all the comfort that there was to say, and the animals silently awaited *first* words of comfort! But he was dry. One part of him wanted to scream: "But the almighty God loves you, will never leave you to be orphans!" while another part of him wanted simply to damn the pack and send it home. As a result, the Rooster said nothing, stared limply at them in disbelief, and became fearfully conscious of his stomachache.

Then, from down below him, from somewhere near the Coop, a voice began to sing a song.

The song was beautiful, a new thing in this place and unexpected. The voice was like a single shaft of cool light through so much gloom. It sang "Ah." It was sure of itself. It wound like a purely silken thread around all the thousand animals in the yard. It rose high and yet higher, singing no more than "Ah." "Ah" to the hearts of the thousand. "Ah" unto their Lord. "Ah" as clear and beautiful as the limber sky.

For one wild moment Chauntecleer thought that this was the voice of the Dun Cow, though he had absolutely no reason to think so. He stared out over the assembly to find her. And he did, at the very back, underneath the trees. No, it wasn't her voice. But once again he saw her eyes with a strange clarity, and he perceived where she was looking. The Dun Cow was gazing directly at the singer. Chauntecleer followed her gaze and saw that it was the Beautiful Pertelote who had begun to sing. The lady had found her voice.

And all the company of the animals was listening.

Chauntecleer sat down upon the top beam of the Coop and found that he was bone weary.

When she had risen to a region of crystal beauty, Pertelote turned her song into "Turalay," and it became a ballad. What a shining and peaceful ballad! It settled the entire multitude and, listening, they closed their mouths.

Yet, in the lovely clothing of this ballad, Pertelote told them what she knew of the danger which was approaching. She told them of the serpents which crawled and killed. But because such knowledge came to them in a song, the animals felt equal to this evil, and they did not panic. She told them of the poisonous bite, the dreadful speed with which they flung themselves. Her ballad did not make the serpents lovely. Her ballad hid nothing of their dread. But the music itself spoke of faith and certainty; the melody announced the presence of God. So the evil which the words contained did not panic the animals, and they listened, understanding. She named Cockatrice

[147]

in her ballad, and she rhymed him with "hiss." And the animals discovered that she had chosen against this abomination and yet had lived; and the animals did not panic.

Chauntecleer looked down upon her of the flaming throat, and he loved her. Mother—no mother anymore; yet she sang. Silent once, but silent no longer; and she sang. O God! Where was there a faith in all the land to match the faith of Pertelote?

And while she sang her lovely melody, for just a moment until it was done, the clouds broke; and then the visible sun touched the tops of the trees, for it shone from the edge of the earth. It turned the white Coop golden; and all the heads of those who listened burned a little bit. And all the ears were filled with light and understanding.

Pertelote finished her song and was still.

Spontaneously in the sun's red glow, in the afterglow of Pertelote's song, the multitude whispered together one massive word: "Amen," as if it were an exhalation from the earth to the spheres. The moment was peaceful and good. In the days to come, Chauntecleer would remember it often and draw strength from it.

But it was soon done.

Suddenly he heard a sound behind him. A gurgling, but more than that: a raging and choking of the waters.

Chauntecleer stood up, looked around—looked and was horrified. During the afternoon of the Council the river had flooded so far abroad that it was now in sight of the Coop. The Rooster's eyes rolled left and right, and the sight was all the same. A sea! The waters looked like an endless sea covering half the earth and reaching toward this place. The sea was all afire. For a mist went up from it, and the setting sun had ignited this mist into what seemed an oily flame. It burned with an ungodly color.

But the horror was not only Chauntecleer's. That strangling sound had caused a thousand animals to stand up, to bob their heads, and to notice for the first time what was happening to the river.

They did not cry out. They stood stunned. They stared. This was the world turning inside out, and they didn't understand. Some would have run away; but in bewilderment they stood still. Some would have burrowed, some flown to the topmost branches. But the lurid sight confused them and they stood stock-still.

Before Chauntecleer could say anything, a commotion began in the middle of the multitude. Politely gabbling from the bottoms of their throats, excusing themselves with many grunts and burps, and stepping on backs and heads as if they were alone in an empty field, the Wild Turkeys had begun to walk toward the river. They had decided to see this wonder for themselves. And, as their eyesight was spectacularly poor, they had to walk straight up to the shore to do so.

But their courteous excuses were lost on the other animals, and their motion sent animals into one another. Fits of nervousness began to explode around them. Tails were stepped on. Here and there someone squealed in pain.

"Where are you going?" Chauntecleer roared from the top of the Coop.

It happened that the Turkeys heard as poorly as they saw. They didn't answer him, but pleasantly continued to step over lesser animals, waddling to the river.

"Where in God's name do you think you're going?" Chauntecleer roared.

One of the Turkeys heard him. "Hada goo-good time, rutabaga Rooster," he called. "Thank you. Goo-goo-by!" He waddled with the rest into the short plain which now divided the yard from the flooding river.

Chauntecleer was confounded.

"Fools! Blockheads!" he roared. "Get back from that water!"

"Thank you, rutabaga Rooster," another called back happily.

The multitude behind the Turkeys popped restlessly. Smaller animals began to be afraid: They didn't know

[149]

what was happening; they couldn't see. They only felt the pressure of big bodies against them. The pressure was growing greater. So they wailed, bit, and began to claw. Greater animals leaped and turned about in confused pain, and the little ones thought that soon they wouldn't be able to breathe. They panicked.

Chauntecleer looked down upon his animals. He saw the whole mass of them begin to boil. They churned, and there was nowhere for them to go. A huge, mighty pinwheel, the congregation started to turn, crying and caterwauling and carrying the little ones under.

"Pertelote," the Rooster cried as if through a storm, "get the Hens inside the Coop!"

Then he crowed a mighty crow for order, but it did no good.

"Scarce," he cried, his voice nearly lost, "tell the animals to look at me! Tell *all* the animals!"

And then, at the top of his lungs he thundered: "MUNDO CANI DOG! CUT THOSE FOOLS OFF BEFORE THEY REACH THE WATER!"

He did not wait to see if he'd been heard. He opened his beak wide and began to crow vespers. Again and again he crowed vespers. Again and again he told the animals, in familiar words, of the night and of the rest which comes with night and of the sleep which follows rest. He crowed as if his heart would break.

One by one the animals began to turn their heads to him.

Mundo Cani had been on the far side of the assembly, farther out, even, than the ragged north edge of the animals. They didn't see him take to his heels and fairly fly around at their backs. The Dog with the enormous nose revealed his talent. He came like the wind, streaking ninety degrees around ten thousand animals, then out onto the plain, baying and barking until even the Wild Turkeys began to hear him. His legs swallowed the earth, and he ran.

But who saw the river vomit bubbles? Who saw the waters roil and rage until they broke? Who saw the river cast up serpents upon the shore? Not the Wild Turkeys. They were half blind, and this was but a pleasant outing. Not the multitude. They had begun to lift their eyes up unto the Rooster, heeding vespers, relaxing. Chauntecleer alone saw them, and he was made sick by the sight; but he never once broke into his crowing to gasp or to plead. Chauntecleer saw the Basilisks—and one other saw them, too. . . .

Mundo Cani hurtled with a speed he could not stop, dead across the plain. But if he could not stop it, yet he could direct it. He aimed his pounding body straight for the group of waddling Turkeys, and he ran the harder.

The serpents burned in the last light of the sun. Damply they slithered to the place where the Turkeys were going. They made dimples in their flesh as they moved.

The first stupid bird reached them, smiling. One serpent bit him briefly in his breast, and the bird died on the spot—a short apology in his throat.

Before another bird could take another step, Mundo Cani exploded in the midst of them. Feathers and absurdly fat bodies blew up in a golden cloud and came down with many thumps upon the earth—yards closer to the Coop. But before they could gain their feet, Mundo Cani had blasted through them once again. Up in the air they went, spinning and squawking; and down they came on their backs and their stomachs, saying, "Oof!" and "Galoot!" Up again and down again, always landing closer to the Coop and farther from the serpents, thoroughly addled and wondering what had happened to the earth. *Boom! Boom! Boom!* Mundo Cani laid into them with all of his bones athwart. On the way to the river they had spent most of the time in pleasant conversation upon the ground. On the way back they spent nearly all of their time bouncing through the air and swearing, decorum forgotten. But they did come back to the Coop, and there

[151]

they lay: bruised, disgraced, fiercely insulted, and alive. All but one, who lay dead near the river.

The serpents had followed for a space. But then Chauntecleer discovered something vital: When he turned his constant Rooster's crow in their direction, they shrank from it. They curled in upon themselves and hid their heads. They knotted together like so many fingers in a fist. So Chauntecleer crowed with somewhat more vigor than one should use for vespers, and the Basilisks rolled back into the river.

But when the serpents were gone, and just as Chauntecleer was about to return attention to the animals, a ghastly word rose up out of the earth. "Wyrm" was the word. Immediately the clouds locked together again in heaven, and darkness fell absolutely.

All of the animals heard the word; it leaked out of every hole in the ground—sulphur, steam, and stench. The odor of rot seeped upward to their bellies. "Wyrm" was the word. It came like disease and hung foul in the air. "Wyrm: *Sum Wyrm sub terra.*" And then, very quietly and very clearly and very confidently, these words: "I am Wyrm, Proud Chauntecleer. And I am here."

Here ends the second part of the story about the savage war between Wyrm's Keepers and Wyrm's minion, Cockatrice.

PART THREE

[NINETEEN] *The Coop-works: preparations for war, together with the most admirable pout of all*

y the middle of the next morning it had become clear to nearly everyone that the Wild Turkeys had decided, to a man, to pout.

As blind and as deaf as they were, they didn't know that one among their number—Thuringer, his name—had died by the bite of a serpent. They merely assumed that Thuringer had somehow escaped the altogether impolite pounding delivered unto the rest of them by a Dog and a vulgar nose. And nobody could tell them otherwise. Therefore they waddled to and fro in the yard holding their ridiculous cornstalk heads high above the animals, *limped* through the yard, and pouted.

And oh, what a pout they could produce!

Chauntecleer had called all the heads of the families to a special meeting near the Coop. This had taken place about a half hour after lauds. The Turkeys, every one, snubbed this meeting—all part of their pout. Of course, they knew about the meeting; and they made certain that everyone else knew that they knew about the meeting: For what's a snub if one hasn't been invited in the first place? They "ga-galooted," and they "gaw-god-awfuled"; they groaned wonderfully and they limped, all within three feet of the meeting place. And they heard not a word of the proceedings.

Just before prime the meeting broke up. Every father returned to his own breed and explained the information and the explicit commands which Chauntecleer had given them. And when the families had learned the parts they were to play in the war effort, they went to work. Every animal in the yard learned a duty, and the crow of prime signaled the time for each to start his duty.

The Wild Turkeys, however, were decided upon a personal duty. Their duty was to pout.

One of them, Corningware Turkey by name, stumbled and flubbered into the Coop itself. Once inside, he slammed the door with a right proper bang. Then he opened the door and stumbled out again, turned around, and slammed the door again. With his bottom wattles stuck out to the distance of a foot, for that is the expression of a pout, he reentered the Coop and banged the door, came out and banged the door, banged the door and banged the door. If anyone passed by, he casually lifted his stubby wing so that his many bruises would be apparent, then banged the door in that someone's face.

It was the duty of the Bees to do something about the loathsome smell which kept seeping out of the earth. Animals had awakened gagging, taking bitter half breaths, retching. As soon as they had learned their duty, the Bees divided into two groups. In force the male drones flew into the forest to search out flowers; they returned each with a sweet-smelling petal. These petals they rained all over the ground before flying back for more. Then the female workers crawled busily among the petals, chewing and chewing them until they made sweet paste, and with that paste they began to stucco the ground over the entire yard. They were making a floor; they were sealing the putrid stench within the ground; they were doing their duty.

So were Paprika and Basil doing their duties. Turkeys both, they sat their crippled butts down exactly where the paste had *not* been spread and would not move for all the

[156]

angry buzzing and exhortation of the Bees. On the one hand, they could not hear. On the other hand, they chose not to see the fussing Bees, for that is the business of a good pout. And on the third hand, they had absolutely no idea why the Bees had undertaken to sticky the entire ground around the Coop. That being a thoroughly empty-headed project (and-and a damn-damn nuisance to boo-boot!), they had decided to sit down upon the clean spots. Be it known that neither Basil nor Paprika nor any other Turkey had a sense of smell. They had strongly disapproved of the generally public and generally impolite gagging that morning.

Finally, the Bees worked around these two and pasted them to the ground. But Paprika and Basil held their naked heads high and pretended not to notice, being quite sure that something discourteous had been done to their bottoms.

Tick-tock the Black Ant was wild with joy; and he said so with extra loud HUPs as he commandeered one division of Ants after another and sent them to their duties. He had never had so grand a host of marching men in all his life. Tick-tock had had his hundred; but he had never had these many thousands, trained and loyal and orderly and polished to a flashing black. For the sheer joy of it, he had them drill for precisely fifteen minutes in the precise middle of the yard before he sent them to their appointed tasks. And then he cried "Dig!" to the diggers and "Tote!" to the toters and "Build!" to the hill builders; then builders, toters, and diggers all went to work, making a thousand ticking noises, as if a thousand bitty clocks were busy on the earth.

Almost before their eyes the animals saw a rampart rise up in a wide and perfect circle around the yard. The Ants made no complaint over the size of their duty. They worked in perfect contentment, and they built a wall, a bulwark of dirt which surrounded all the animals and finally stood as high as the gracious antlers of the deer. All around the outside of this wall they dug a trench quite as deep as the wall was high. And into the wall they buried here and there a Turkey up to his neck. Ants argue with no one if there is some way to keep schedule and do duty in spite of him. They didn't mind the Turkeys' pout. They didn't mind the Turkeys' plopping themselves upon the rising wall. And they thought that the naked little heads which finally stuck out of that wall were rather ornamental, if somewhat irregular.

The Turkeys, of course, pretended not to notice that they were up to their necks in the sod. The most wonderful pout of all is the kind which is snooty. It notices nothing at all—and so is noticed by all, as it were, by accident. It says—all unintentionally, to be sure: "You don't care about me, world. Well, then, go your way. Don't bother to notice how much you don't care about me. I don't care two sniffs for you. Tit tat. Tit tat. Tit for tat." The entombed Turkeys held their heads high and won a second victory by not noticing the streams of Red Ants which marched over their eyelids, bearing food to the animals within.

Chauntecleer believed that, since Red Ants were mighty tiny, they would be in less danger than anyone else outside of the camp. Therefore he sent them to gather food. The enemy might see a corn kernel moving across the ground. But who could see the tiny Red Ant underneath it?

There is an ancient saying concerning foxes which Lord Russel was glad to quote to anyone who had the time to hear it. It went this way:

> *Foxes detest*
> *The odor of rue;*
> *Therefore they guess*
> *That others do too.*

Lord Russel himself most particularly detested the strong, bitter scent of the rue plant. For that particular reason alone he rubbed his paws vigorously in its oils; and most generally, when he was going about his foxing trade, he stank of the plant.

Now, because Chauntecleer believed in Russel's stealth, he and the others of his breed had duty as sentries. The foxes crept through the plain which divided the dirt wall from the flooding river and they kept watch against the enemy. Chauntecleer also believed in their inbred sense of personal safety. He knew that in the moment when these foxes spied an enemy *outside* of the camp, they would be *inside* looking out.

As he scrambled from bramble to bush, now, Lord Russel, the Fox of Good Sense, stank fearfully.

But Turkeys have a most impartial sense of smell. The Turkey Fry noticed nothing unusual about Lord Russel, when he took up his pout next to this Fox, except that Russel's movements were somewhat unpredictable:

Lord Russel hid behind a bush.

And then he hid behind a bramble.

And then he hid behind a Turkey.

And then he hid behind a bush—

Back in a flash to the Turkey! That was the best cover he could find and it cast the best shadow.

When Lord Russel observed that his present cover was alive, he considered what to do and decided upon giving the creature a proper greeting.

"It is, or so I would say it is and I would, *er*, suppose that the majority of clear-thinking individuals would be inclined to, *er*, agree that it is—which I say with the understanding that you are a clear-thinking fellow—a fine day."

Zip! The Fox was away to a bramble. *Zip!* The Fox was back to the Turkey. Both bramble and Turkey were brown; but the Turkey was immeasurably the better company.

[159]

Slowly the Turkey Fry turned his head around to look upon this wonder.

"Galoot," he said in a wounded voice, referring to his tail feathers, for these Lord Russel hid behind.

"To the point!" the Fox exclaimed. "I am my, *er*, self of the same trenchant, not to say, incisive, and, or, trenchant opinion."

"Galoot," said Fry, turning fully around and pointing to the bruise on the top of his head.

"A modification not to be, *ahem, ahem*, dismissed."

Lord Russel did not notice the bruise. Nor did he speak to it. Rather he took the time to quote at length for Fry a short poem about Foxes and rue. And then the two of them entered upon a stimulating conversation, and one Turkey lost his pout. He became polite again. He had found, among the thousands of animals, a kindred spirit.

But another Turkey, the magnificent Ocellata, was not so wishy-washy in *his* pout.

The magnificent Ocellata, let it be known, made an art of superb politeness. Ocellata had manners. He excused himself even to the trees—when he could be sure that it was he, and not the tree, who had bumped into the other. And what a mannerly excuse he made of it! First the great loop of flesh which drooped over his beak began to shiver with pounds of humility. Then his chest puffed out like a pillow, all so that he could bow to the tree. And then, as he bowed, the little beard which grew out of that chest would brush the ground. All the world said: "What a bow the magnificent Ocellata can make!" "A-polo-polo-pologies," Ocellata would gabble to the tree.

But let this same Turkey consider himself to be insulted, let him feel that he had been injured in his dignity, and then woe! He made an art of the pout!

Fourteen times—he had counted them—fourteen times last night a Dog with an enormous nose had booted him high into the sky. Ocellata had tried to reason with the creature, for that was only in his nature. In his politest voice he had said, "Galoot." But what good did it do? When one says "Galoot" from ten feet up in the air, with his head down and his feet uppermost, who is able to hear that one thinks someone ought to apologize? And then when one has hit the ground with a twenty-pound thump it is very hard to say anything at all. His conversation has come to an end, cut short! That is, without a doubt, an insult to one's dignity. A Dog might at least have said, "Excuse me, Ocellata," But no Dog had said such a thing (never minding the fact that Ocellata was stone deaf). And that is, without another doubt, excellent grounds for a pout.

The magnificent Ocellata pouted, and that right at the source of the indignity.

After a long investigation, he found out where this Dog was lying in the camp, and he took up his pout nowhere else but there.

"POUT!"

Mundo Cani heard a noise. He raised his sorrowful eyebrows without moving his head and noticed that there was a Turkey in his neighborhood. This Turkey was scratching furiously at the ground as if the ground were hateful. He was muttering to himself violent, unseemly words: "Galoot! Galoot!" He was shaking the loop of flesh which overhung his beak. And he was eating pebbles as if they were berries.

"Oh, some food! Galoot food!" the Turkey muttered. "Oh, some day! Galoot day! Oh, some company! Galoot company! Oh, some world! Galoot world! Galoot, galoot, galoot world!"

Mundo Cani was inclined to agree with this speculation about the world. He heaved an everlasting sigh, which blew seven Bees out of range without his meaning to, and rolled his eyes to watch the Turkey. The sight alone caused him untold guilt. But he looked at Ocellata anyway.

"One does one's work in the galoot heat of the galoot

[161]

day. Without complaint! Oh, some day! And who has bruises all over his body? And whose poor muscles ache? *One's!*"

Such fine chest hairs this blessed creature has, thought Mundo Cani to himself.

Then it dawned on the Dog that the Turkey was eating all the pebbles which lay in a straight line to him: If the Turkey continued as he was going, he would soon be at Mundo Cani's tail.

"Then I am in the way," Mundo Cani sighed. "Always I am in the way." These words brought him very close to tears. But he controlled the impulse and moved his tail so that it stuck straight out behind him.

Without a blink and without a pause—as busy as the next one in the yard—Ocellata changed directions and continued to aim for the tail, swallowing pebbles and mumbling.

Mundo Cani thought that perhaps he should say something to announce his presence in this place. But the Turkey was so busy that he was ashamed to interrupt him.

He moved his tail again. Again the muttering Turkey changed directions. And he was getting closer.

There was nothing left for the Dog to do but to pretend that he was not there. So he pretended with all of his might that he was not there. And he watched while the Turkey swallowed up the last pebble before the tip of his tail. The Turkey, being so busy about his work, did not stop. His next mouthful was a tuft of Mundo Cani's hair.

"Oh, some food! Galoot food! Foul, hairy food!"

Great tears rolled out of Mundo Cani's eyes and made pools in the dust on either side of his nose. But he was pretending that he was not there, so he only sighed and was quiet and watched the oblivious Turkey.

The Turkey took a mouthful of tail hair. He ripped a mouthful of rump, he pulled a mouthful of back, a mouthful of withers, a mouthful of neck. The water streamed from Mundo Cani's eyes and nose. But he lay still and said nothing. He was very, very sad: a Turkey on his back.

Master of the Universe, *why* did he always have to be in the way of everybody?

The muttering Turkey took a bite of hair from the top of his head—and then, suddenly, he was eyeball to eyeball with the Dog. He stopped and gave Mundo Cani a piercing stare directly into his left eye. Mundo Cani looked back and wept.

"Oh!" cried the magnificent Ocellata without moving an inch. "Are you here? I di-di-didn't notice you!" he shouted.

"On account of I am not worth the notice," said Mundo Cani Dog.

"But by goo-good manners," shouted Ocellata, "I, for one, know that someone should say excuse me." The Turkey then pealed: "EXCUSE ME!" at the top of his lungs.

"You're excused," said Mundo Cani.

But the Dog spoke to Ocellata's rear because the satisfied Turkey was already waddling away. It had been a most admirable pout. Pebbles rattled in his crop as he waddled.

Then Mundo Cani couldn't help himself. The word came out of him altogether on its own: "Marooooooned!" he wailed piteously.

Several hundred animals in his area stopped work, looked, and then wondered at the hairless stripe up his back. And Chauntecleer, who had been overseeing the creation of the animal camp, walked over.

"It's shaping up, Mundo Cani Mutt," he said cheerfully. "There's a place for everyone, a job, and every family is settling in. And the food is coming and the stink is going and I'm right pleased—"

He stopped. He glared at the Dog. Mundo Cani was weeping without an end.

"What's this?" the Rooster hissed.

[163]

Mundo Cani shook his head.

"Why, you're a pump! You're a running pump! Who flushes you every time I look around?"

"Ah, pump," the Dog managed to say; and then he delivered himself over to heavings of the breast and sobs.

Chauntecleer glanced quickly around. Two Turkeys were waddling over to begin new pouts. The Rooster flew at them and aimed them elsewhere in the yard. He returned to the Dog.

He put his beak to Mundo Cani's nose.

"Weep yesterday!" he hissed. "Weep next year. Weep with your fat head beneath the river. But don't weep here and don't weep now!"

"Ow-oooooo!" Mundo Cani's chest convulsed. It had finally happened. The dam had broken loose inside of him; sorrow burst out everywhere; and nothing in this world could plug it.

"Of all the—" Chauntecleer choked. And then he jammed his wing down Mundo Cani's throat.

"Dog, do you have any idea what's going to happen tomorrow? A war! A violent, bloody, murderous war! Serpents are going to fling themselves against our wall. They're going to reach into this place to kill what lives here. And this poor squad of animals is going to have to fight. Do you think they'll fight tomorrow if someone panics them today? They need great hearts. But you! You'll bleed dry every heart in the yard! I don't want it, Mundo Cani. Do you hear me? I don't want to hear drip out of you. Is that clear? Let them eat today. Let them sleep tonight. And then tomorrow we may have something to say to the enemy."

Chauntecleer looked closely at Mundo Cani. He held his gaze steady for a long time. Then, when he spoke again, his voice was less thorny, more level, and much more kind.

"Mundo Cani Dog. You saw, and I saw, and no one else saw, what is to come. You saw the damnable vipers, the

[164]

slick candy shapes. You saw them nip Thuringer unto his death. And did you hear the name given to the deep root of this evil? His name is Wyrm."

The Dog closed his eyes. He struggled mightily against his sorrow. His mouth was dry. Feathers make a mouth dry.

"We alone have seen this thing," the Rooster said. He tested the Dog: Slowly he began to withdraw his wing. "Mundo Cani, I need you. You know what nobody else knows. You witnessed the death and you did not run away, but you became salvation for a flock of fools. You have a great heart, Soul of Mine; and I need you. Who else can run like the wind? Who else possesses such a talent? One day, years and years ago, God tossed a blessing to that nose, and that nose was big enough to catch it."

When the wing was pulled all the way out of Mundo Cani's mouth, many long sighs followed after. Little feathers puffed out with the sighs and curled through the air. But no weeping came out. All of the sobs had gone home into the Dog's breaking heart.

"Good, good, good, Mundo Cani," Chauntecleer encouraged him. "Good, Soul of Mine. Hush. Be at peace."

He stood up, wiping his wings together like towels. And then he saw the Dog's back.

"Who bit you?" he demanded.

Mundo Cani turned his head away.

"Do serpents bite? Who bit you!"

Mundo Cani looked back to the Rooster and shook his head. He did this because he could not talk, yet. He also did it because it really didn't matter who had bitten him, serpents or otherwise.

Chauntecleer was about to lay his head back and crow for the Weasels, now his police force. But before he could, Mundo Cani placed a paw on the Rooster's back and beseeched him with his eyes. The Rooster reconsidered, stood still, and waited.

It was a main struggle, for his throat was lodged full of

[165]

lumps. But when he could finally speak, Mundo Cani put his eyes down and said: "A Dog came here. A Dog brought you evil. A Dog is going away."

At first Chauntecleer was going to laugh. But in a rush laughter was drowned in irritation, and he became instantly angry. "One lout of a Dog!" he said.

"Will my Lord look at himself?" Mundo Cani said woefully. "Here are two eyes that should have gone to sleep two years ago. Are they sleeping? Instead they spend time on a Dog of no value. Here is a voice that one night hallowed a lonely Dog when he cried outside the door. How does this voice sound today? It has worry in it. The worry makes it hard. It has sorrow in it. The sorrow makes it break. And it is as tired as the two eyes. A Dog saw these members when they were God's miracle. But a Dog brought God's curse into the Coop. Curses are maybe stronger than miracles. Such a Dog should be dead. He is going away."

Chauntecleer was dumbfounded. "Listen," he said, stamping the ground compulsively, "you go away and I'll follow you! I'll wart your nose. I'll break it! What damn-fool talk is this? You think *you* caused all of this? Are you the father of Wyrm? You blithering nincompoop! You utter fool!"

Mundo Cani said it softly, looking into no one's eyes: "The Master of the Universe is embarrassed that he made such a mistake as this one—"

"Cock-a-mamie!"

"—and he wants to cover it up."

"Cock-a-balderdash!"

"It is my fault, my Lord."

"BULL! BULL, YOU PLUG-HEADED DOG!"

Mundo Cani sighed. He shook his head and sighed again. He tried to speak, but failed miserably. He waved a paw in front of his face as if that would say what was on his mind. And then he spoke in a baby's breath, confessed:

"On account of this Dog—here is evidence, my lord—on account of this Dog, a beautiful Turkey, banded and brown, died last night. Ah, this Dog did not save him. And he died."

"That's your evidence? That! Why, you alone—"

Suddenly Chauntecleer threw himself away from Mundo Cani. He strutted up and down the camp, jerking his head and flaring his neck feathers. He was swearing. Little animals scurried out of his way. Other animals who had been taking a rest leaped up and hurried back to work. John Wesley Weasel, who was about to report a quarrel between the Ducks and the Geese, looked at the Rooster and immediately decided to report nothing at all. Chauntecleer came to the wall, then spun on his heel and raced back to the Dog—a thought in his brain.

"What has that Cow been saying to you?"

Mundo Cani said, "My Lord has a right to laugh at me."

"Your Lord! Your Lord has a right to stuff you! What did that Cow say to you yesterday? Did she saucer your mind? Did she convince you of guilt? Is that how she explains an evil?"

"Yesterday evening there was a Turkey—"

"Yesterday, Dog, there was a Cow standing next to you in the back of the assembly. Once she sat with me, but then she said nothing at all. She talked with you. What did she say to make a miserable fool the more miserable?"

"My Lord must be right about something. When did he ever make a mistake? But Cows don't take the time to talk with this Dog. There was a Cow?"

"There was a Cow!" Chauntecleer exploded. "I thought her something good. But now I think—"

All of a sudden, Chauntecleer sat down. His wings hung loose to the ground. His neck sagged. His eyes showed an infinite exhaustion. A trembling Rooster faced a sad, sad Dog.

"Hear this, Mundo Cani Dog," he said. His voice was

like sand. He put his two wings on either side of the Dog's great nose. "If it is God's curse which a Dog brought with him into this Coop, then a Rooster needs the curse of God. Can you believe this? If it were a bushel of fleas which a Dog brought with him, then this Rooster would be happy for a bushel of fleas. A Rooster needs a Dog. A Rooster has come to love him. Stay."

For a long, long time, while the business of the day went on round about them, Chauntecleer looked at Mundo Cani Dog, saying nothing. And then he laid his head down across the Dog's great nose. And because he was so passing weary, the Rooster fell asleep that way, and he dreamed no dreams.

So how could Mundo Cani go away then—or even move?

[TWENTY] *The night before war—fears*

When Chauntecleer woke up again, it was midnight and he was in pitch-blackness. Several times the Rooster opened and closed his eyes, but he couldn't tell any difference: It was all darkness. On this night not even stray light reached the earth through the clouds; so tight, so heavy were they in heaven, that Chauntecleer felt their weight on his back, and he groaned. The whole earth, and especially this round camp on the face of it, was in a closet—muggy, still, and absolutely dark. And the closet door was shut.

Chauntecleer didn't want to move. He felt surrounded by the invisible presences of his animals; he didn't know where nor how to move. From every direction: grunts, coughings, snorts, sighs, rustlings; now and again a dream shout from across the camp sent ripples of worry everywhere; legs, claws, snouts, and jowls nudged the ground nervously; back to back the animals surely lay, and that wakefully—an impossible and dangerous maze. Volatile. Chauntecleer didn't want to move. . . .

But "want" and "won't" are two different words.

". . . run away! Now or later, it don't make no never mind. Now's the better."

Chauntecleer's ear went sharp. Under the general restlessness of the animals and through the night he heard spoken words. Someone was holding secret conversation in hoarse bursts of whisper.

". . . seen him? Seen this Cockatrice or his . . . ?"

"Never seen . . . ! Flank nor feather, beak nor claw . . . no knowing what kind of . . ."

". . . Beryl! Oh, Peck, *her* I seen!"

Peck! There was a name. So these two were members of the Mad House of Otter. Chauntecleer stretched his ears to hear, but lost most of their words. Yet the tones of their conversation he caught very well, and he didn't like the sound of it.

". . . horrid! Nothing natural, not natural-born . . . a broken neck like that! Shoulda seen, Peck; a blow so strong . . ."

". . . the gash on Ebenezer Rat! What about that? What about that? Scrape, what're we gonna do about that?"

"Me, I'm . . . place."

"You what? But Chauntecleer—"

"Hush up, Peck! What do you think? The camp's got ears!"

Then Peck very earnestly asked a question which Chauntecleer lost altogether, and Scrape gave him a long answer. It was obvious that a plan was hatching, growing out of the grisly fear of the two Otters, and that Peck, though he wasn't sure of its righteousness, was surely interested in the length of his own neck.

Again and again Chauntecleer heard the name Cockatrice pronounced in dread:

". . . don't *know*, Peck! And you gonna go against that? Die, Peck? For what? A pack of softhearted . . . ?"

One by one Chauntecleer heard other voices join the whispering.

". . . away? Tonight? . . . can't see nothing, Scrape!"

". . . defend . . . own territory."

"But . . . !"

"Oh, let the Rooster watch out for himself!"

"Cockatrice! Cockatrice! *Cockatrice!*"

Now even those animals who did not talk were stirring—restless, hopheaded, filled with strange imaginings, scared. A general groan began to spread from the Otters' muttering; widening circles caught ears, thumping hearts, bristling hair into them. In a moment the animals would begin to stand up, and then what? The night was dreadfully dark. The camp was dangerously crowded. And tomorrow! Every creature needed his rest tonight. More than that, every creature needed desperately every other creature at his side tomorrow—

Chauntecleer broke his silence and stood up. He fought an urge to excoriate these rotten renegades, these traitor Otters: Scrape should be skinned!

Instead, from the place where he was, he began to crow compline, the seventh holy hour of the day. Cool, smooth, restrained, a silken lariat, the Rooster gave his animals, in the darkness, a point of recognition. He covered them with the familiar. He announced his presence. Then he drew them back from the edge. He blessed them right gently, crowing nothing of the battle for tomorrow—but naming every one of them their names. Names, one after the other, with a prayer for the peace of each one: That was compline on this particular night.

Soon the restless animals on every side began to settle down again. Their own names in the Rooster's mouth had a transfiguring effect:

"Nimbus," Chauntecleer crowed, "the Lord's peace is with you."

And Nimbus the Deer, whose flanks had begun to shiver, who was jerking his head, ready at a crack to leap and flee, Nimbus heard his own name in the mouth of his Lord, and he came to his senses again. Dark was suddenly not so dark anymore. He lay down encouraged—for who had known that he was so well known?

"Pika," Chauntecleer crowed next, and behold! Nimbus was himself the more encouraged to hear the name; for Hare Pika, whom he could not see, was suddenly with him, a part of his company. Name followed name. Lonely was lost in communion: The company grew as if lights were turning on. And Nimbus the Deer went to sleep.

[171]

So it went. All the animals began to believe in sleep again, and the dark camp settled down.

But as he crowed this remarkable compline, Chauntecleer the Rooster was walking slowly through the camp straight for the Mad House of Otter.

And when he came to that place, he didn't stop crowing or lose a breath for compline, but, as if it were by accident, he stepped up onto Scrape Otter's back and stood there, crowing and twisting his claws into the Otter's fur.

Scrape grunted. The Rooster gripped the tighter.

Scrape began to whine. The Rooster made a vise of his feet, then spread his wings, took three enormous flaps through the air, and dropped the Otter bang among the Weasels. Scrape had no doubts about the cause of his punishment, though not a word had been spoken to him. And when Chauntecleer had finally climbed to the top of the circular wall, he crowed, "Scrape! The blessing of the Lord is on you—even on you, Otter!"

An Otter decided to forgo his plan; and, finally, he too went to sleep.

There were thousands of names to be crowed. That was good. The night was very long, and Chauntecleer needed the names, for compline tonight should last the whole night through.

The Rooster walked along the top of the wall, crowing—gently giving ease to the animals' sleep, but himself gravely worried over the weakness of his army. That's why he could not stop crowing. The Otters' plot had made him wary. The quick deterioration of the camp, their readiness to chuck and run, had been a revelation to him. Their fear of the enemy had become his fear of them; and for him, as well, the enemy became the more frightful. So compline was a necessary lie. It was peace spoken to the fearful. But it was also one fearful himself who crowed that peace.

[172]

It was a long, long night before the war. It was an exhausting compline.

Only once during the night did something break the rhythm of his crowing the exceptional compline. Toward morning.

It began with a laugh.

High in the invisible sky above him, Chauntecleer suddenly heard malevolent, screaming laughter—so cold, so evil, so powerful a bellowed laugh that he gasped and forgot his crow. His feathers stood on end. All the darkness around him swelled with the hateful sound, and the Rooster stood perfectly still.

"Ha! Ha! Ha!" screamed the sky laughter. It was distant: It came from just underneath the clouds. But it fell with murderous bullet force. It seemed that the mouth of the laugher was aimed directly at him. Then Chauntecleer's heart stopped.

It knew him! This laughter knew Chauntecleer, knew exactly how he was standing, knew the fear driven into his soul, knew him for a weak commander, knew him lost, dead, and buried.

"Ah, ha! Ha! Ha!" It stroked its victory there in the sky—pleased laughter; strange, insidious, watchful laughter. . . . And suddenly Chauntecleer had no idea where he was. On the wall, to be sure—but where on the wall? The side near the forest? The side—God forbid it!—near the river? He had been walking the wall for hours, heedless, crowing; and a circle is a circle. He *was* lost! And right now it was vitally important that he know his position. Damn the darkness! How could he give a bold front to the devil above him *if he didn't know where he was?*

That one knew, and he didn't. That made the Rooster naked!

So Chauntecleer spun on his heel and began to race back along the wall. Not outside the wall he ran, for what would he find there? A ditch, and then what? Forest?

River? Not down into the camp. The animals would hinder him, trip him up.

On and on around the wall he ran, he rushed, headlong, hearing his own breathing and breaking his lungs for breath; hearing the hard, delighted laughter above him. Through the black night he ran, and he began to whimper: "It's here! I want to see. I want to see. I want to see. O God, where am I?"

Then, blindly, he ran straight into a soft flank. He yelped, then tumbled off the wall, down into the ditch.

The Dun Cow followed him down, and once there she breathed on him. Immediately poor Chauntecleer drove himself like a child into her neck, curled, and gave himself over to the refuge. He had absolutely no doubt who she was. And, strangely, her presence did not surprise him. Neither did he stop for his own dignity. Simply, he was thankful for the shelter, and he hid himself there, and he waited for the trembling to quit.

When the Rooster's reason had come back again, he discovered that the laughter was gone and the night silent once again—save that he heard wind in the trees of the forest. Trees! Ah, the Dun Cow had brought him down on the north side of the wall; the camp stood between him and the river, and he was relieved. And he knew where he was.

Chauntecleer lay a long while against the fine fur of her neck. He let his mind free to think of the night; and soon his mouth was free as well. He found that he was talking his thoughts aloud. The Dun Cow listened. Low and long he shed his private fears into her silence—all of them, right up to the final idiocy that he, Chauntecleer, Lord and leader, should be reduced to racing wildly in circles! Long and low he shared every piece of apprehension with the Cow who lay beside him in the ditch, and this, too, relieved him.

But then, even in this special hour, a tiny thing began

to nag the Rooster: that the Dun Cow, who had filled Mundo Cani's ear yesterday with such a steady stream of talk, now was saying nothing at all to him.

"Speak to me," he said bluntly and loudly in the night. "Have you nothing to say to me? Who are you? Why are you here? Where do you come from?" And then, a question which Chauntecleer never formed on his own, nor ever would have asked, had he thought about it first: "—Why do I love you?"

His own question so shocked him that he shrugged his shoulders as if there were light in the ditch and he could be seen, as if to say, Forget it: I didn't mean it. And he consciously shut his mouth and said no more.

So the last hour of the night passed by. Once or twice he felt—just barely—the prick of her horns upon his back. They kept him wide awake. And in that time it seemed to Chauntecleer that the Dun Cow *did* speak to him, though he could never remember the language she used, nor the timbre of her voice; and she did not offer any answer to any one of his questions.

But what he learned from her made his spirit bold and his body ready. Three things she gave him: weapons against the enemy. And two he understood immediately. But the third remained a mystery.

> *Rue, she said, protection.*
> *Rooster's crow, confusion.*
> *One thing else to end the deed—*
> *A Dog with no illusion.*

Shortly the Dun Cow was gone again, and the Rooster alone in his ditch. And then, with a faint light to make shadows of every solid thing, the night was done and the dire day had begun.

[175]

[TWENTY-ONE] *Morning: rue and the Rooster's crow*

he sky was a stone—hollowed underneath, hard, pure white, hot, a lid locked over the whole earth. Never before had the sky been so white. Never before had it turned the heat back onto the earth with such ferocity. Neither blue nor pink, neither soft nor kindly, but white, hard, and hot, this sky, and angry.

A hissing sound seemed to come from all around the horizon, where the stone lid trembled and heat escaped like steam.

There was no sun. The sky *was* a sun. And this day did not dawn. It hit the earth with a fury. It struck every animal in the face. It woke each one with pain and with the sound of hissing.

Children stumbled and could not stand. Mothers and fathers found that their legs were sluggish. When they reached to help their children, it was with a maddening, slow motion that they reached. Everyone's thoughts turned unto himself, and he wished for one cool drop of water to loosen his thick, sticky tongue.

The animals began to moan, and would have moaned forever like the sick, except that a thought crept into their minds:

They said, "Where is Chauntecleer?"

Now their eyes began to peel open in spite of the white light. They looked up on the wall which went all the way around them.

They said, "Where is Chauntecleer? Have you seen Chauntecleer? Did he crow the morning lauds? We haven't heard him crow!"

They stood up on their shaky legs to look around. The children, who did not open their eyes, felt their parents' bodies move and depart, and they began to whimper. But the parents looked closely at the wall, and they did not see Chauntecleer on the top of it.

Some thought that they could remember Chauntecleer's crowing in the night; but they were not sure. And no one had heard him crow since the morning began.

Close to panic, they said, "Where is Chauntecleer?"

And then someone said, "He left us!"

Again the animals stared wildly at the wall. It was true. Chauntecleer was not on the wall. The Deer shuddered and stamped their feet. The Rabbits sat up straight and froze at the thought. The heat was heavy on them all. They trembled.

Someone else said, "He left us! He escaped in the night! He saved himself and left us to die!"

The animals began to walk around aimlessly, sweating. They shook their heads against the dismal, universal hissing. Oh, God, the livid sky!

Then someone lost all patience. "Traitor!" he cried.

Immediately John Wesley Weasel screamed, "No!" He was running, dodging through the crowd, trying to force his way up to the wall. He would say something, if he could get somewhere to say it.

"He betrayed us! He locked us in! He called it a fortress! But it's a prison!"

"No! Is no!" John Wesley cried, darting, scrambling, driving for every snatch of open space he could see in the crowd. Who said these things about the Rooster? Was an ass! John Double-u would find him, would bite the tendon in his heel, would bring him down and shut him up. Was an ass! If only John Wesley could get near to him to see.

All of the sweating animals moaned, "A prison!"

They began to surge toward the wall. John Wesley was lost.

Why did the Wild Turkeys go first up the wall? Had

[177]

panic pierced their ears? Did they run on their own? Or were they driven, helpless foam before a groaning sea?

The Wild Turkeys fumbled up the inside of the wall, falling and rolling and rising again. When they reached the very top of the wall, they suddenly began to shriek in mortal terror. They turned around, tried to fight against the coming crowd. But it was useless. The animals no longer knew them. The Wild Turkeys wanted desperately to be back inside the camp again, but who would let them?

Then the Turkeys went mad. They whirled around, jittering hideously and screaming.

This the animals *did* see—for the Turkeys were wrapped in serpents. Glistening, deadly vipers entangled their legs and gripped them at the throats, coiled their bodies and waited a teasing moment before the bite.

The entire camp of animals fell into a ghastly silence, watching the sad dance on the top of the wall.

And then the Turkeys threw back their heads, and they died, making a gargling sound in their throats before absolute silence.

There was no sound but the hissing. Basilisks hissing.

The dead bodies fell out of sight over the wall. But two of the Turkeys happened to fall inward. They tumbled into the camp. The serpents with burning, lurid eyes slithered off the dead; and the animals, with wild, staring eyes, made room for them, backed and backed away.

These serpents put their heads up, so that as much of their slick bodies stood up off the ground as crawled on it, and they drew away from the two dead Turkeys. They fanned out in several directions, approached the staring animals, crawled slowly, their damp bodies dimpled with light and making wrinkles, their eyes burning a mordant fire, their heads high and proud like little kings, their mouths grinning and hissing.

But the animals stood mute and could not move. Neither could they tear their eyes from the Basilisks.

[178]

Suddenly Chauntecleer crowed from the top of the Coop.

The serpents stopped and twisted their heads, looking.

Chauntecleer crowed again—mightily, dangerously, purely.

The animals found their legs, rushed, and stampeded away from this place, some crying out for the first time.

Chauntecleer crowed again. He made a whip out of his crowing, and he lashed the serpents with it.

The serpents withered, shrank back. They rammed their heads against the ground as if they would crawl into it; but the floor which the Bees had put there held tight against them. They began to stream for the wall.

"I adjure you by God," Chauntecleer crowed—conjured. "If ye be above or if ye be below, that ye go hence!" Such was the cut of his crow.

In a twisting mass the serpents worked their ways to the wall. The animals pressed against the Coop at the Rooster's feet.

"I adjure you by the most great name, go hence! If ye be obedient, go hence! If ye be disobedient, die! Die! *Die!*"

Up and over the wall they crawled. And then none could see them but Chauntecleer, for he was on top of the Coop. *Rooster's crow, confusion*, the Dun Cow had said. Chauntecleer had just practiced the third category of his crowing, new learned. The occasional crows and the canonical crows were nothing, now. These were the Crows Potens!

Up and over the wall, however, they all crawled but one. This one serpent had burrowed deep into the bowels of the Turkey which it had killed and was well hidden. This serpent hid inside of the magnificent Ocellata. This serpent was still inside the camp.

"In God's name," Chauntecleer spat at the animals huddled so tightly around his Coop, "what is the matter with you? Didn't you hear me yesterday? Did you forget everything?"

[179]

The animals put their heads down and stood still, trembling.

In the doorway of the Coop stood three figures apart: John Wesley Weasel and Mundo Cani Dog, both of them out of breath; and Lord Russel the Fox with a grotesque, painfully swollen muzzle. Behind them was a huge pile of rue.

Failing everything else before, John Wesley had leaped the wall and shot into the forest to find Chauntecleer. At his warning Mundo Cani had carried the Rooster back into the camp with an amazing speed.

"God give the lot of you brains!" cried Chauntecleer. "Or not one of you will be left alive. Did you suppose the wall was a joke? Do you think I laugh at you with what I do? I knew the serpents were out there!"

Chauntecleer stared at his animals, furious. Almost to himself he said, "We're going to fight an enemy; but first we will deliver ourselves into their hands." Then he shouted: "You invited them into this camp! Do you know that? Not just by climbing the wall. Not just by making doorways of your bellies. But by your faithlessness. Warriors! Warriors? Rabble and children, the whole lot! If you don't believe in what I say, if you don't hold together, there will be slaughter! Who wants to go home now? Get out! Get away from me!" Chauntecleer cried—and immediately he was ashamed of his outburst. This was a difficult moment for the Rooster. He glanced at the Turkeys already dead, at the animals already humiliated, pawing the ground; and he felt that he had gone too far in his anger.

A moment to control himself, and then in a quieter voice he commanded that every child and every mother of children be moved to a special place toward the north of the camp.

Then, while that was being done, Chauntecleer took

[180]

himself into the Coop and stood facing a blank wall for a full ten minutes. Not a Hen disturbed him.

"The rue," he said finally to Pertelote, even before he had turned to look at her. And when he did turn, it could be seen that his face was calm.

"Rub rue everywhere around the place of the mothers and children. Make a closed circle of it. But see that you keep enough back. Every warrior should also be smeared with the stuff. Every warrior should stink of it." And then he went outside.

Rue, she said, protection.

The serpents had been able to approach the camp wall without notice, that morning, simply because the guards— the Foxes—had been no longer on watch, and there had been none to cry warning. When the Dun Cow had left him, when the white morning had just begun to break, Chauntecleer had seen an appalling sight. He had seen the Basilisks begin to break water at the river's edge to blacken the beach—thousands upon thousands, wriggling and creeping into the plain.

Chauntecleer had leaped to the wall, prepared to rouse the camp and to bring Russel back. But first he saw a marvel: Every tree, every bush upon the plain, was withering and falling sere before the Basilisks—every bush except one! This bush they avoided. "Russel!" Chauntecleer had cried. Immediately the Fox shot from that bush and began to run for the wall. The bush withered in an instant; but Russel the serpents did not yet attack. And Russel, against all sensible principle, opened his mouth and snapped at them. He caught three serpents in the middles of their backs and kept running. They writhed around his snout, and he stumbled and fell into the trench at Chauntecleer's feet—but he bit them, and they died.

It was when Chauntecleer helped the Fox—stunned with pain and swelling frightfully around his nose—that

[181]

the Rooster noticed the bitter smell of rue which cloaked his guard.

Rue, she said, protection.

"The wonder is," Chauntecleer said now to his warriors as they stood tight around the Coop, submitting to the vigorous rubbing which Pertelote and the Hens were giving them, "the wonder of it is that they can die! Know that. Repeat it to yourselves. Believe it. Never, never let their strange shapes cloud your minds or persuade you otherwise: They are vulnerable. They can die!" Chauntecleer was making his last, preparing speech before he sent his warriors over the wall.

He began in a low, intense voice to scourge his warriors. He leaned down from the top of the Coop and scraped their souls with a description of the evil outside the wall. Not the Basilisks alone he described, but evil. Evil itself, and what it can do.

Then, in precisely the same voice, without the least comforting transition, he began to name their children. The contrast was tormenting. It produced—without the word ever being spoken—the word "death" in every heart.

The warriors great and small, with many teeth and few, began to cast eyes toward the wall. Their teeth ground together. Hoofs, paws, and claws began to scratch dust. Nostrils flared.

Still in the same voice Chauntecleer gave over the names of their children and began, rather, to name his own. He called each one of the Three Pins "Prince." He pointed to the place where these lay buried. "Mine," he said. "Yours," he said in that low and lashing voice. "But mine are no longer and yours nevermore."

And then he named the name of the adversary. "Cockatrice," he said, so quietly that he could barely be heard. "Cockatriss. Cockatrissssss."

A deep rumbling rose up from among the warriors, and as it did, Chauntecleer drew out the hissing of the enemy's name like spitfire, louder and louder, until above the rumbling he arched his neck and he screamed: "COCKA-TRISSSSSSSSS!"

Fur stood up like needles on a thousand backs. Muscles twitched violently. Hackles were raised on every feathered neck. Teeth came bare. Lips curled back in a thousand snarling faces.

Chauntecleer's low monotone had driven outrage into the souls of his warriors. It had also restrained them, holding them taut, quivering at his feet. Now he threw it away.

"Up!" he roared, and the traces were loosened. "Go!" he cried, and the reins were dropped. They were free. They turned away from him. "Now God goes out before you! But you! You! Kill them utterly!"

Not fast, but with a dreadful purpose, the warriors moved to the wall. Chauntecleer set up a startling, brilliant crow from the top of the Coop—the Crows Potens—and he watched.

The serpents on the other side all put their heads up, waiting. It was as if all the field between the river and the wall had suddenly sprouted living heads. The heads, like fingers out of the ground, waved back and forth; the flesh gleamed. The hissing sprayed the air, loud, louder, deafening.

All at once Chauntecleer saw a horrifying sight. On a mound by the river he thought he saw himself—like a mirror of himself. He saw a Rooster of grim appearance, a Rooster covered all over with scales, grey scales down the neck and underneath the chest. This Rooster had a powerful, twisting serpent's tail and a red eye. Level, cold across the plain, the eye was looking back at him. Cockatrice, too, was watching.

If it had been more than that instant, if Chauntecleer

[183]

had thought about what he saw, he might have learned a lesson and abandoned hope on the spot. For there was not one enemy, but three, and each the greater, each the father of the other. And each one wanted the blood and the very soul of the Rooster. And each would have his day: the Basilisk, then Cockatrice, then great Wyrm himself. This, the Rooster might have known, was only the beginning!

But the Rooster did not choose to know. He turned his face and crowed.

[TWENTY-TWO] *The first battle—carnage, and a valorous Weasel*

how Chauntecleer crowed then!
He ripped his eyes from this Cockatrice he had never seen before. He heard one low, guttural laugh below the hissing. Then he turned attention to his warriors and crowed with a will.

The battle began.

Over the wall the Red Ants streamed, like pouring sand. They went among the Basilisks and bit. It was a stinging bite; but every Ant, when he had bitten flesh, died. Yet his body clung to the place where he had bitten. The serpents writhed. The hissing became a screaming and a curse. They waited no longer. Serpents flowed forward to meet the attack.

Now the warriors of size burst over the wall, crying, galloping, roaring, raging. Great animals raised a battle cry. They tossed their heads. They thundered their hoofs among the serpents; black blood spurted onto the land. But the larger serpents doubled themselves with taut violence; they fired themselves into the air, arrows; they flung their bodies like ropes around the necks of these animals. They squeezed tight until the necks broke and the noses ran red blood.

Small animals took the serpents into their mouths and whipped their heads back and forth to snap the backs of the enemy; but then they spun in circles, shrieking, as the serpents' poison burned through their bodies. The birds swooped down from the air, vicious claws open, piercing, breaking the flesh of the serpents. The Foxes beat left and right with sticks, leaping backward whenever a serpent drew near enough to touch. Their sticks dripped black blood and smoked. The Foxes were quick. They used their tails to turn corners at a sharp angle. When a serpent reared at them, they snapped their tails left, then left with their whole bodies, and the passing stick cut another in two.

But the Basilisks made sharp points of their own tails. They sprang from the earth and sailed through the air tail first like darts. They stabbed the hearts of many creatures. The smallest serpents stung furry animals between their toes; then these animals would curl into shivering balls and plead for someone to chop their feet away. Others clawed at their own skulls until the skin flapped, because the poison had ascended to their brains.

The Sheep had thick, woolen protection over all their bodies. But their eyes were open. The Basilisks flew at their eyes.

The Otters fought together. The Weasels fought, each one of them, alone. But the Weasels fought! Most furious and deadly and courageous of all. So fast their sudden speed across the ground, so quick their cut and their retreat, that the serpents could not watch for them.

The Rabbits were there: That alone was their courage. They died easily under the serpents' bite, legs jerking as they did.

The battle was a long one. The field ran wet with blood both black and red, so that the animals slipped in it, and some who lost their footing came to grief.

Oh, there was a screaming and a busy grunting on every hand across the plain. Animals went forward with their shoulders hunched, their heads down, their eyes stern and dirty. Everywhere the serpents slithered, hissed, and bit, innumerable. And Chauntecleer heard it all from the top of his Coop. He saw it all from his high place. The tears broke from his eyes, and he wept.

But yet he crowed, and he crowed as though his heart would break. Hatred, God's curse, sorrow, and Godspeed he crowed together in a constant, burning beauty. The Crows Potens. And never once, never once in all that time, did he take his eyes from the battlefield.

Then a small figure came to the top of the wall. He came from the bloody plain. Once on the wall, he turned and stared at the fighting. He was breathing hard, winded. But soon his breath came in strange jerks. His whole body began to quiver and shake. After a moment he threw back his head, and it could be seen that his mouth was wide open. It was John Wesley Weasel. And he was laughing.

"Ooo," he laughed. "Is going, going! Cut for cut! Kill for kill! Serpents wants fighting? Hoopla! Ha, Ha! *Gets* fighting! Furry little buggers knows how to fight, hey?"

He thrust the air a couple of times with his legs. Then he turned and came down into the camp.

There was blood on the left side of his head. It matted the fur, and a swelling had closed his left eye. Also, his left ear was gone. He had lost it to the battle, and now he came for salve to stop the bleeding. If he lost too much of his blood, he would become useless to the fight, and that would have greatly irritated the Weasel.

"Ho, Chauntecleer! Ho, Lord Chauntecleer!" he called as he neared the Coop. "The Rooster sees the way it goes?"

Chauntecleer thought: Yes, I see the many dying, see the slaughter. But he was crowing heart-bloody crows and could not answer the Weasel.

"Is blackguards, Chauntecleer. Is filthy blackguards from hell. We kill them. Double-u's makes the field stink with them!"

They kill us, Chauntecleer thought behind his crowing. Savagely.

"Crow, Lord Chauntecleer!" the Weasel cried buoyantly. "Crow like judgment day! Hears you!" he cried; and he went into the Coop by the Widow's back door.

In the minute while he was gone, Chauntecleer saw a Deer go down to his knees in the vermilion mud. The Deer Nimbus raised his face to heaven, and then he died without a word. There was a serpent lodged in his breast. Chauntecleer crowed. He crowed and crowed.

Suddenly he felt the Coop tremble beneath him. Though he was crowing loudly, yet he heard a storm of shocked, painful curses come from down below. Immediately he thought of Pertelote inside. But he couldn't leave his place, and he couldn't stop his crowing.

Then John Wesley burst out of the back hole, a writhing serpent in his mouth. John Wesley slammed the serpent violently against the Coop. Again and again he whirled the serpent until the body ruptured and spewed black blood everywhere. And still he battered the ragged body with great blows. He tore at the dead flesh. He dug at it with blinding speed and with loathing.

He stood back. "God! God!" he cried, wringing his paws. Then he ran back into the hole.

This was the Basilisk which had hidden itself in Ocellata's body. This one had waited his time before sliding into the very Coop of Chauntecleer.

John Wesley came out of the hole again, tenderly bearing the body of the Wee Widow Mouse. He walked to the Coop door, and he stood there, crying: "Pertelote! Pertelote! Come and see what they have done!"

He cried: "Chauntecleer, this is what they are doing. What does Mice do? Mice cleans in the spring. Mice wears aprons and sweeps. But the damned—! The damned—!" He said no more.

Pertelote came to the door. She took the dead Widow from the Weasel.

He said: "See what they are doing."

[188]

He stood and watched while Pertelote found a place for the Widow within the Coop. Then he filled his lungs to cracking, and he screamed: "Do and do and do! John Wesley will do for you!"

In a flash he had cleared the ground between the Coop and the wall. Up and over the wall he sped. He leaped the trench and threw himself bodily into the war.

How the Weasel fought then!

Here was a serpent raising its head. John Wesley shot by and took the head with him. Here a serpent flew through the air. John Wesley darted off the ground, caught it; when they hit the ground again, the serpent was dead, bleeding at the eyes. Here was a tangle of serpents all leeched to a Fox's back. With a cry John Wesley pounced. He snapped and slaughtered them all. John Wesley was faster and more fierce than fire. He pierced through the battlefield crying, "Do and do and do!" On the left hand he killed a hundred as if they were paper. On the right he killed five hundred. Many, many perished before him. But he was not enjoying his carnage. He was enraged. "Do and do and do for what you have done!"

The animals saw his stark fury, and they took courage. They roared. They turned, every one of them, and pressed a wild attack toward the river.

The serpents hissed and tried to meet this thundering wall.

The river belched forth bales of ready Basilisks. But the animals were convinced: Serpents could die! As one mighty beast, with John Wesley at its head, the animals came forward killing. Dying and killing.

Chauntecleer crowed. He crowed lustily. He stood on the tips of his toes. He stretched his neck and crowed almighty power to his warriors.

"Children!" Another voice! Another scream not Chauntecleer's!

Suddenly the Rooster was gaping. He saw his mirror on

[189]

the other side of the field. He saw the scaly, serpentine Cockatrice.

"Children!" Cockatrice put out his wide wings and lunged into the air. Higher and higher he circled, his tail curling out behind him—ascending until he was at a point above the fighting Weasel. Then he dived.

"John Wesley Weasel!" Chauntecleer shrieked.

The Weasel dodged. But Cockatrice only skimmed the ground and rose up again on his great wings. Again he gained height, then stooped and dived again at the Weasel. He aimed his tail from underneath his body like a stinger.

John Wesley scrambled. He raced back and forth. There was no fighting for him now—only the running to escape.

Down came Cockatrice, a bolt of lightning. His tail opened a wound on the Weasel's side; and again he soared up to the white sky.

The Weasel was busy running. The battlefield was nothing but flat open spaces. No place to hide. No time to dig. Just running, dodging, and running again—while Cockatrice screamed out of the sky yet a third time. Suddenly the Weasel felt very tired. He thought that he would stop running soon.

Animals and Basilisks both had ceased their fighting. Basilisks because their numbers had been decimated; those left were slipping toward the river. Animals because they were horrified by the scene before them and helpless.

On a whim Chauntecleer looked to his right. There, far away across the plain, he saw Mundo Cani coming, head low, beating the earth with his feet, running. "Oh, run, Dog!" the Rooster crowed. "Run! Run!" Mundo Cani had seen the trouble.

Again, Cockatrice was falling from the white sky like an arrow. The Weasel was bustering around the field, veering left and right to make a difficult target of himself. But if this caused trouble for the dropping Cockatrice, it also troubled the Dog. Mundo Cani was fast flat out. Already he had halved the distance. But how could he veer with the Weasel?

"Russel's bush!" he roared to the Weasel without slowing his course.

John Wesley stopped dead, looked at him, surprised.

"Run!" screamed the Dog. "Oh, John! Run!" Cockatrice was taking level aim.

The Weasel ran. He made a pattern of his sudden, jagged running. He glanced at the Dog, gauged his speed, then stared at the place where the bush used to be.

From the top of the Coop Chauntecleer saw a Dog of enormous speed and a Weasel of quick turns close in on one another. At a certain spot they met; and then the Weasel was no longer visible. Cockatrice drove himself into a lump of earth.

Mundo Cani made a wide, pounding circle and returned to the camp.

"Home! Home! Come home!" Chauntecleer raised his voice again to cry retreat to his animals. It was time. "Home! Home! Home! Home! Home!"

And they came. Shaggy, sad, small, and stumbling, they came. In the instant of the retreat, insufferably weary; dragging, shambling; hurrying more against their fatigue than from the enemy; stunned, they streamed back—the Dog foremost of them all. They mounted the wall and fell into the camp, damp, sick, sorry, and alive.

The day was ending. The hot day was nearly over. The night was at hand. Here and there on the camp floor lay the broken animals, too tired even to consider that the battle had been theirs. They slept and did not sleep at once. Just—they were there, and that was all. Inert.

Chauntecleer, still on the top of the Coop, gazed at them and choked on his love for them. The strain of the day had left him soft toward his animals.

[191]

And while he looked, he heard a very weak but bitter voice nearby the Coop. The voice said: "Tell a Dog to put me down. John's wet, he is."

In spite of himself, Chauntecleer let slip a sudden, stupid giggle. Then, in a manner more grave: "Mundo Cani, it's over for a day, don't you know?"

"Is *ways* to bite a Weasel," the Weasel said, and then he passed out. He looked like a wet rag hanging out of either side of the Dog's mouth. Blood dripped from the point of his nose and from his tail.

"All this time you've been standing there?" Chauntecleer wondered, for it had been a while gone as the animals found places inside the camp.

Mundo Cani's eyes were filled with anguish. They looked mournfully up to the Rooster. Who knew how kindly the Dog's tongue was licking John Wesley's wound on the inside of his mouth?

"Well?"

The Dog laid the Weasel gently on the earth and sighed.

"Chauntecleer!"

Like an iron arrow the cry came to him.

Chauntecleer spun around. He saw the battlefield moist and glutted. He saw wreckage. He saw bodies in which there was no life. The field everywhere was still. So who called to him?

"Chauntecleer! Proud Chauntecleer!"

From across the entire battlefield came the poisoned voice. Standing on an invisible island out in the flooding river, Chauntecleer's mirror was crying challenge. Cockatrice. His tail twisted powerfully and dashed the water as he called. His red eye watched the Rooster unblinking. His voice was slamming into Chauntecleer's face:

"What are animals? No account! What is a battle won with numbers? Nothing! What is a commander who hides behind a wall? Let the commander show himself tomorrow. Cockatrice will meet him—and him will Cockatrice kill!"

Chauntecleer's mirror slipped into the water and disappeared. Chauntecleer watched that place until the ripples had played themselves out, and the river became smooth in the evening. Battles, battles—how many to make a war? And when you have won one, then what *have* you won?

The Beautiful Pertelote stepped out of the Coop and looked up at her husband. He didn't see her. He was grieving. He was listening.

Another voice arose from the soil itself, a voice confident and mild. It said: "Behold the Rooster who suffers much more than he must. Ah, Chauntecleer, Chauntecleer. Why do you suffer today and tomorrow?" oozed the compassionate voice. "Curse God. Curse him, and all will be done. Or, lest you forget the truth of things, remember: I am Wyrm. And I am here."

And then, finally, it was the night.

[TWENTY-THREE] "We fight against a mystery"

efore and after, and a battle in between. The night before the battle had crackled with energy and fear. But this night afterward fell loose to the ground in exhaustion. Animals took no care where or how they lay. They sprawled everywhere.

Here and there a head rose from the ground, snapping at the air; a cry trembled on the night; a leg began to thrum and jerk violently. Once John Wesley Weasel begged vengeance for the death of the Wee Widow Mouse; then Pertelote sang to him and soothed him back into silence. But silent or screaming, neither one made any difference to the Weasel, because he was sleeping and did not know what he was doing.

As if it were the earth itself underneath them all, or the wind around them all, a groaning never ceased the whole night through. This was the voice of the wounded; they could not take breath or release it except in pain. Even as they slept, they groaned.

From the top of the Coop, at the right time, Chauntecleer crowed a short, bitter compline—very much like a growl. And when the ceremony was done, the Rooster, too, was done. In silence he descended from the Coop; he walked among his animals, climbed the wall, turned once to look the whole camp over, then disappeared down the other side.

The night was not altogether dark. Some grim, shadowy light touched things. So Pertelote had seen the Rooster leave. She had been watching him ever since the retreat, never saying a word or asking one of Chauntecleer. But now she felt a deep compulsion to follow him outside the camp.

She knew that he wasn't coming back in again. Today all the warriors had fought; tomorrow it would be Chauntecleer alone. This knowledge had driven him out, for already he was effecting a separation between himself and them. This knowledge he carried while he wandered through the stiff field beyond the ditch. And this same knowledge drew Pertelote's heart after the singular Rooster.

She followed Chauntecleer's path among the animals toward the wall. She climbed the wall and made ready to go over, just as Chauntecleer had done. She tried—but in that moment, for the first time, her courage failed her. She stood still.

Poor Pertelote! For a long time that night she struggled with herself, hesitating between the camp and the battlefield, loathing herself, yet loving her life too dearly to trust it to the darkness. Some light there was, to be sure. But it was the *darkness*, the nothingness in front of her, which struck fear into her soul.

The light which so thinly illuminated this night came not from the sky but from the river itself: strange light! A smoky glow hovered just above the water; a softly flowing sheet of bloodless light stretched as far as the river went. It was light barely seen, fatuous fire; but it was enough to make the battlefield seem a black, bottomless pit.

That pit, that mouth in the earth—*that's* what frightened the Hen. She knew perfectly well that there was firm land under the blackness. And yet she feared that once off the wall she would fall and fall forever.

Strange light. Stranger darkness! And the warm, familiar camp behind—this was the confusion, the struggle

[195]

which rooted Pertelote's poor feet to the wall and would not set her free to fly.

Oh, but somewhere in the darkness was her husband, her Chauntecleer. . . .

"Chauntecleer," she whined softly. At least she *thought* it had been soft. But he must have heard her.

"Get back!" he barked, bodiless in the night. "You've got no business up there, Pertelote. Get back into the camp!"

That broke the spell.

Her first impulse was to focus on his voice, to know where he was. But her second impulse was the swifter; it was to become suddenly, hotly, angry with the Rooster. And at the third impulse Pertelote took to her wings and flew straightaway from the wall.

Instantly the wall, the camp, the animals, the Coop, and everything else was swallowed up in darkness. She came from nothing. She flew over nothing. There was nothing ahead of her. She felt no motion in the flying, because nothing showed her that she moved. Only—there was the dim, smiling light above the river, white, shapeless, smooth, and soft. That was the only something in all the world around her. All the rest was chasm. All the rest was pit—horrible, hopeless blackness!

"Ah, God," she said, stabbed with panic at her foolishness, beating her useless wings. Where was she to go? She tried to fly straight up. But suddenly she herself was nothing anymore. For one small second between wing beats, she truly thought that she had died.

"Pertelote, you fool!" Chauntecleer's voice! Again, it broke her.

She simply quit flying, folded her wings, fell out of the air, and hit the earth.

"I told you, didn't I? I said you had no business out here. This isn't for you, idiot! Nor for anybody else. I'm the one—! WHERE ARE YOU?"

[196]

Pertelote tried to stand up on shaky legs, and slipped. The bloody earth. She did stand up, and then she stood stock-still, looking around. Some shapes on the ground were coming visible to her, though they were only blacker forms in the darkness. This was a foreign land, and she was very lonely in it.

"All right, then," Chauntecleer shouted, "where are you? Let's get it over with and be done." He was quiet a moment. Then: "Pertelote! For God's sake, where are you?"

"I'm here," she said.

"Where?"

"I don't know. Here."

"I'm coming to you," he shouted, and she nodded.

There was a long silence, and then Chauntecleer shouted from a different place: "Listen, how am I supposed to know where you are? Make a noise."

"Here," Pertelote said. How terribly lonely she felt!

"Good! Keep it up."

"Here. Here. Here. Here," she repeated, singsong. The word grew ridiculous in her mouth. "Here. Here. Here." Maybe to give it some meaning, maybe to make a responsible adult of herself once again, Pertelote started to walk—whether toward the camp to avoid the Rooster, or toward Chauntecleer himself, she did not know. Her loneliness in this place was stunning her.

The ground was uneven, and the darkness around her feet total. She tripped. Her face slithered into the mud. She lifted up her head, sick with the smell of blood; her eyes saw a dim sight; and she was horrified. Two inches away from her own face was the open mouth of a Deer—neither speaking nor breathing. It was open as in a scream, but it screamed no sound at all. The Deer was dead.

Pertelote gagged, stumbled to her feet, and backed away. Again she slipped and fell, this time to rise from the mud gasping, like someone drowning. She plunged away—and Chauntecleer grabbed her.

"Now!" he said. "You tell me what you're doing out here."

For one moment the Hen was rigid. In the next she seized Chauntecleer and drove him with an incredible force back toward the Deer. Loneliness had split open in rage.

"What's his name?" she demanded.

"What?" Chauntecleer was overwhelmed. "I don't know," he said. "I can't see."

Pertelote pushed him closer. "Touch him. Feel his face. Tell me his name!"

"But he's dead."

"I don't care," the Hen fairly screamed. "I want to know his name!"

Chauntecleer reached through the darkness and felt the Deer. He drew back, then, until he was standing right next to Pertelote. In a stricken voice he said, "Nimbus."

"Nimbus!" cried the Hen. "His name is Nimbus! Nimbus, too, is dead!"

"Pertelote—" Chauntecleer tried to say, but she spun away from him.

"I will give you my children. I'll sit with a suffering Fox. I'll patch you a Weasel. I'll sing to him. I'll even watch you leave the camp without a word to me—and I will endure. Stop! Listen to me! You will go out and you will fight with Cockatrice and you will die, and I will endure. This is the way that it is. You choose. Fox, Weasel, Chauntecleer, Lord and Rooster—you all of you choose; and I am born to endure. But who is Nimbus? Oh, God, why does he have to die?"

"Pertelote, I didn't—"

"Let it end, Chauntecleer! With Nimbus let it end right there. He's the last sacrifice, the most stupid! Nobody knows who Nimbus is. Well, then he's a child to me—my

[198]

husband and my father. And he's the last that I'm going to give!"

Chauntecleer put a foolish wing around her shoulder. "You can't talk this way. Not now." But Pertelote wrenched herself free.

"Get away from me, you! You've already left me. So! You've gone to fight the Cockatrice, my Lord. You're dead already. So! So! I go to mourn Nimbus."

She began to run through the darkness. Chauntecleer made no attempt to stop her, nor even to follow her. But his head fell back and he wailed in pain: *"Pertelote!"*

Immediately, as if shot, Pertelote collapsed. Right where she was in the muddy field she began to weep loudly. The sobs were ripped from her soul like roots from the earth, and Pertelote cried. "Oh, Chauntecleer."

And so he came to her, and this time she let him hold her. Among all the black forms on the battlefield, these two made one small incidental lump—but this was a living lump; that was the difference.

After an age had passed Chauntecleer said: "Pertelote, I love you."

"I can't do it anymore, Chauntecleer," she said gently, in her own voice. "Twice I've seen the Basilisks. Twice the destruction. And Cockatrice—he never, never goes away. I'm tired, Chauntecleer."

"So am I," he said.

"I thought we won today. But I thought I won nine months ago when I fled by the river. Marriage and our children—I thought these were victories. But Cockatrice came back, and he comes back, and he comes back; and now he wants you, too. There should be an ending."

"There will be."

"But what *kind* of an ending? You will die, and then what? When will I die? Oh, God, I should have died a year ago."

"Pertelote, it's not written that I must die."

[199]

"So you say. So you say. Chauntecleer, you have never been close to Cockatrice. God help me, I have."

To this Chauntecleer had no answer whatever. He held his peace.

She said, "Who is Wyrm?"

Chauntecleer said truthfully, "I don't know."

Pertelote made the question more difficult: "Why is Wyrm?" she said.

Chauntecleer began to chuckle, and the Hen was surprised. "Ask me why is Mundo Cani's nose," he said. "I don't know why that boot was born into the world, but there it is. I don't know, Pertelote. I don't know."

"What is Wyrm?" she asked.

"Oh, Pertelote. Have I seen him? Do I know his father or his mother? Has he told me his shape or his purpose? Has God ever explained to me what lives beneath our feet or why he permits it to be? I've asked him often enough, Lord knows. But he never answers. Wyrm is. How shall I say what Wyrm is?"

"Beyond everything else we fight against, there is Wyrm. Beyond the Basilisks. Deeper even than Cockatrice—Wyrm."

"Even so it seems to be."

"Then we fight against a mystery," she said.

"Yes," he said.

And she said, "Chauntecleer, I am so very tired."

The loose light above the river rolled and seemed to form itself into shapes—grinning, confident faces billowing across the water. Against that unholy light Pertelote saw Chauntecleer's silhouette. Then her thoughts passed from herself to him, for she saw how sadly low his head was bent. And Pertelote was changed.

"Chauntecleer?"

"What?"

"And I love you."

Now the Rooster found a fine hold on her body and

[200]

squeezed her so tightly that she grunted.

"Oh, Chauntecleer, I have such a very little faith," she said.

"But you came out to this wretched place," he said. "Who else came out to find me?"

She searched to see his eyes and failed. Only his comb like a crown was visible against the river's light. "Do you forgive me?"

"Ah, the lady with a flaming throat, who sings like the spheres, who weeps and sings again, the lady who endures forever—she asks me whether I forgive." He touched her gently. "What else is there, Pertelote? I forgive."

"Will you fight with Cockatrice tomorrow?" she asked. Perhaps she finally wanted all things properly in place by his speaking them: It was an honest question.

"Yes," he said.

"Such a thing is possible?"

"Such a thing will be. I am not going back into the camp until I have fought him."

"You have chosen against evil."

"I have."

"And perhaps my husband will die for his choice."

"Even so," he said. "We fight against a mystery."

[TWENTY-FOUR] *The second battle— Wyrm's Keeper and his minion in the sky*

So peaceful the morning that dawned, then. Mist on the river hid it, and there was quietness there. Mist filled the round wall of the camp, so that it was a bowl filled with drowsy white. Quiet white, because the invisible animals slept. Mist floated among the tree trunks in the forest. Mist floated across the battlefield like the train of a white gown. So gentle the day. And the sky, so benevolent.

So insidious, so foul the lie!

Pertelote alone was visible. She was a rag left sleeping on the wall. Her head lolled over the edge in loose fashion; her wings had lost strength and fanned away to either side of her; her beak was grimed, dusty, because she had literally fallen asleep in the middle of a watch. For a little while she had no idea that the morning was upon her. Her sleep was a blessing, for just a little while.

Suddenly a sound went up from the hidden river and blasted her awake.

One note. One long, eternal note so cold, so drilling, so fierce with hatred, that Pertelote reeled backward. If the sound had broken off, she might have frozen in her attitude. But it didn't. It kept on blasting, and Pertelote began to run away. She ran, broken and crazy, beating the dirt with the ends of her wings, snapping feathers. She

[202]

rounded the wall toward the forest, pumping her small head, breathing through her nose.

Her eyes rolled wildly in her head.

But a second sound trumpeted from the forest, shrill, unearthly. It hit her full in the face and with such sudden power that the poor Hen crumpled down and covered her head.

The river sound trebled, shrieking fury like the winds of a tornado. The sound from the forest echoed that and shook the trees. One, and then the other. The ground trembled. One, and louder still the other. They clapped together over Pertelote, and she began to pray.

The mist was everywhere calm. Invisibly the voices searched one another, fought one another.

Then Pertelote began to recognize one of the sounds— and she was filled with wonder. Slowly, slowly she lifted up her head. She looked toward the forest. Then she sat up, astonished.

There, on the topmost limb of the tallest tree, stood Chauntecleer, his wings wide like an eagle's. He was crowing lauds as lauds had never been crowed before. The tree dipped and swayed from the impact, but Chauntecleer rode the motion and crowed: Lauds was his challenge to the hidden fury of the river, to Cockatrice.

Pertelote's vision became intensely clear now. She *saw* the Rooster, his high head, his golden breast, his azure legs. And she could see, bound tightly to his spurs, two savage spikes.

"Gaff," she breathed into the splitting sounds of the morning, "and the Slasher. He's put on Gaff and the Slasher!" Thus the names of the Rooster's weapons, old weapons.

Pertelote wanted to weep.

But then the river sound began to change. Pertelote whirled around and saw Cockatrice burst out of the white mist. He swooped low for a moment, crying his own hateful lauds, writhing his tail into devilish, impossible shapes. Then he gave power to his wings and soared up and up, stretching his neck and screaming, until he was but a dangerous needle in the sky.

Blitzschlange! Cockatrice had become the *Lightning Snake*!

Pertelote turned to Chauntecleer's tree, and then she cried, "Don't! Chauntecleer! Chauntecleer! Don't!" But who could hear her? The challenge must turn to fighting now. Lauds was over.

Chauntecleer had also leaped into the air. He sank some way, but then his wings caught at the air, grabbed at it, and lifted his body up above the forest.

"Oh, for the love of God!" Pertelote pleaded. "Chauntecleer, don't!"

But who could hear her?

Chauntecleer bumbled upward. There was no doubt that he could not fly as the *Blitzschlange* could, that Cockatrice! Roosters do not belong in the air. But he had ceased his crowing and bent his energies to the flight. He rose higher and higher above the forest, putting space between himself and the ground. He went to meet the enemy.

There was only one sound now. Cockatrice lay on high and laughed! Cold, evil, powerful his bellowed laughter! He had contempt for the Rooster laboring to meet him. And he seemed almost to be still, so high was he above the earth. He seemed to have found a windy shelf up there, and from there he spat at Chauntecleer.

But then the *Blitzschlange* slipped the shelf. That devil tipped forward, made a dart of his beak, a rod of his tail, and dived.

Down he streaked out of the sky.

Pertelote lifted a wing, as if she might protect her husband.

Chauntecleer saw him coming and changed his course. He flew no longer up, but straight forward.

But Cockatrice only bent his dive as if it were a gleam-

[204]

ing, flexible saber. He ripped the air, faster and faster. He was a bolt, an arrow; he was lightning. The little needle grew into a spear, an axe—and he hit the Rooster full on the back!

Chauntecleer fell.

Cockatrice spread his powerful wings and sailed up and up again to a greater height.

Pertelote watched the Rooster tumble from the sky; but he was fighting the fall. He tore first one wing and then the other out of the wind; then, by main strength, he spread them out again and caught himself. Soon his fall began to slow. He made a level flight of it, and he flew just above the treetops. He was in control. Pertelote started to breathe again.

Cockatrice, a little dot near heaven, laughed; he saw what Chauntecleer was doing. But Pertelote began to strike herself on the breast because she, too, saw what Chauntecleer was doing.

He was flying upward, struggling upward again.

"Come to me!" screamed Cockatrice from his enormous height. "Come to me, Rooster, and I will give your flesh back to your own beasts, and they will feed on it!" He circled near heaven and laughed like a demon.

But Chauntecleer answered nothing. Silently he labored higher and higher, the one living thing in all the middle sky.

The mists of the morning were gone, burned away by a white sky; and the air was glassy clear. Nobody had heard the animals waken, yet there they were, one thousand faces rounded by a wall, watching their Lord as he lugged himself higher above them.

Suddenly Cockatrice's laughter broke off, and he attended to business. The dot cried, "Then I will come to you!" And he pitched down out of the sky.

Chauntecleer worked hard. Again he laid his flight flat over the earth, but again it was useless. Faster than thought the demon dived. He didn't check. He didn't swerve. He went straight at the Rooster and cracked into him with all of his falling might.

Pertelote jumped at the sound of that hit. This time the Rooster did not catch himself. He fell. Turning over and over, his loose wings doubling backward, a chunk of feathers in disarray, Chauntecleer fell out of the sky and crashed into the forest.

Pertelote did not know that she was beating her breast. Neither did she hear the pleading, mewing sounds coming out of her own throat. Nor did a single animal in all the camp move. Their eyes were at the forest, seeing nothing.

Cockatrice sat on the top of the sky once again. His wings were tireless.

Then Pertelote wailed: "Not again!"

Out of the forest, crippled in his flight, Chauntecleer was rising up again. With much trouble he cleared the treetops. He hung midair for a moment. Then, thrumming his weary wings with a great deal of wasted motion, he turned his flight upward again—a sadly broken flight. He slipped and flew, slipped and flew. He fought his way—but he went up.

This time Cockatrice waited. This time Cockatrice forced the Rooster to go higher than he had ever gone before. But the Rooster pounded the air, and he *did* go higher than he had ever gone before. He made no sound. Neither did the demon above him. Cockatrice cried no challenge. He bided his time and waited.

The third flight lasted forever.

Then Cockatrice was waiting no longer. Everyone was watching; yet no one knew when the dive had begun. Deadly, and as silent as time, Cockatrice hurtled from the roof of the sky.

Who was left to believe that Chauntecleer could escape the plunging *Blitzschlange*? But yet everyone pleaded in his soul, wished that Chauntecleer would try, would dodge.

But he didn't. The Rooster hung still upon the air as the demon closed distance, shooting at him. Nor did he even straighten his flight. As if in a dream he regarded Cockatrice; and then, just before the murderous strike, he rolled over on his back with his claws above him.

Crack!

The collision echoed through the forest, sent ripples across the river, and caused Pertelote's heart to break.

But this time the Cockatrice did not find his own wings. He did not rise up again. He was bound to the Rooster, and they fell down together. They whirled together to the ground—then hit with such force that they bounded up again, and only stopped rolling at the wall of the camp.

Pertelote stared, transfixed.

Chauntecleer lay underneath—Cockatrice, his winding tail, on top of him. Gaff had pierced Cockatrice at the throat. The Slasher was buried deep in his chest. Cockatrice was not dead; but he was dying. Yet his hatred for the Rooster was so intense that he did not back away nor pull the weapons out of his body. Instead he lunged forward, reaching with his beak for the Rooster's neck.

He thrust Gaff entirely through his own throat. The point slid bloody out of the back of his neck. Jerk by jerk he pressed the Slasher ever deeper into his chest. He inched closer to Chauntecleer's face.

Chauntecleer only held his legs above him, a barrier, and watched the cold red eye. Watched the beak slash and snap at him.

The demon's face was just in front of his own—a mirror.

Then hot blood burst out of Cockatrice's mouth, spurting and steaming, and the demon died. Beak to beak, his red eye open, the dead stared at Chauntecleer; and the Rooster vomited.

In thorough disgust Chauntecleer heaved the body over. He yanked the weapons out of it. He ran a short distance, then stopped and drove his beak into the ground, squatted, and slid his chest and both sides of his head against the earth to clean the filth away. Spasms shook him. He vomited again a thin bile. Then he went limp and stood with his head bowed, exhausted.

For a moment there was utter silence. Pertelote had never moved from her place on the wall. The animals were glaring at her back, waiting for some gesture to tell them of the events outside the camp; but they saw none—only a Hen absently beating her breast.

But the answer came.

In a rasping, tormented voice, Chauntecleer began to crow the crow of victory. So the animals were set free. They climbed the wall to see what he had done; and when they saw, they were astonished by the thickness and the strength of the demon's tail. But still no one said a word. Chauntecleer was not done.

Slowly he returned to the body, gargling a vehement, crazy crow. Savagely he began to hack at its neck, ripping the skin, exposing veins and cords and a dark green meat. The animals turned away. Chauntecleer, it seemed, had become an offense. Into his own beak he took the bare neck bone of the enemy; this he shook with such violence that it broke and the head came away from the body. Chauntecleer raised this head high, and walked.

Across the battlefield he walked. Around the corpses he walked. Wearily, but with the head of Cockatrice above him like a standard which trailed torn flesh, Chauntecleer walked to the river.

At the shore he stretched his neck and cried out: "Wyrm! Oh, Wyrm! Oh, wretched Wyrm! Swallow this thing and gag! Your Cockatrice is dead, and I have done it!"

Then he threw the head with its open eyes into the water. Like a stone it sank, and Chauntecleer watched with satisfaction the long string of blood which followed it down the water. Done. He started to go home.

He was halfway across the battlefield when he heard a

new noise behind him. He turned, and all unconsciously he groaned. Waves of sorrow nearly drowned the Rooster, because he saw that the waters of the river were seething. Where the demon's head had entered them, the waters were boiling: Bubbles broke the surface in a steady, restless rash; then the boil spread wide, and the whole river itself was churning.

"Chauntecleer! Chauntecleer!" cried the voice from underneath the ground. "The last sin is the worst. How vain to kill the Cockatrice. But how much more contemptible to glory in an empty thing! Chauntecleer! *I am Wyrm!*"

The waters began to crawl up onto the battlefield, closing like fists around the large corpses and lifting the little ones up. For three days the river had held to this shoreline; but no more. The river was rising again, spreading itself toward the camp.

"*I am Wyrm!*" The voice issued from every pore in the ground, a stinking violation. *"And I am here!"*

Suddenly Chauntecleer took dizzy and began to sway. How many battles make a war? How much, and how much more, can a Rooster bear before the break? He let his slack wings touch the ground on either side of him so that he wouldn't fall altogether, and then he dragged back to the camp. But again and again he turned his head to look behind, trying to believe what he saw.

He stumbled into the trench at the bottom of the wall. Slowly he raised his eyes. There was Pertelote, still standing on its top and looking at him. Chauntecleer shrugged his shoulders and tried to smile. He spread his wings empty in front of her. The smile didn't work. It hung all too crooked on his face. "Do you know? Do you know?" he said as if he were very young. "Pertelote. I don't know anymore," he said, and then he fainted. Many of his bones had been broken.

Chauntecleer had won. Chauntecleer was victorious, but

[TWENTY-FIVE] *The Hen, the Dog, the dun-colored Cow*

ut it is entirely possible to win against the enemy, it is possible even to kill the enemy, and still to be defeated by the battle.

Chauntecleer had not lost his life to Cockatrice, but he'd lost something infinitely more dear. He had lost hope. And with it went the Rooster's faith. And without faith he no longer had a sense of the truth.

When the battle with Cockatrice—sore, exhausting battle—turned out *not* to be the final battle after all, then it was Wyrm and not the Rooster who rejoiced in victory. With seven words Wyrm had more than weakened him, for he was already weak. With seven words Wyrm had made the war an endless thing and every victory a joke. With seven words Wyrm had murdered hope and sent the Rooster mumbling through the windless halls of despair. And with seven confident words Wyrm had struck down the leader of the land, so that the land was no longer proof against his escape. Leaderless, loose, the Keepers would lose their strength. The bond was breaking, the patch frayed at the center of it, the prison gate unlocking. And Wyrm saw freedom in front of him!

For Chauntecleer one thing and one thing only held any meaning now: his own feelings. All of the rest was mere shadow—smiling, mocking shadow.

When he swam to awareness again, Chauntecleer discovered that he was in the Coop on a clean bed of straw. He tried to move, but he couldn't. His whole body—the bones within and the flesh without—was stiff, wooden.

All of the sights and the sounds around him washed into one another, so that he thought he was seeing everything through a sheet. Someone, he thought, had put a sheet over his head.

He considered this sheet for a moment. "Muslin," he thought to himself. "No, not muslin. Something sheer, something thin and light."

The color of the sheet kept changing, flushing red every time his heart beat and deep crimson when he breathed, almost as if it would blot out all things else. Chauntecleer thought that this was both kind and remarkably beautiful, and for a moment he took pleasure in it.

But only for a moment. Soon the fact that the sheet was over his *head* struck him with a deep and piteous sorrow.

"They think I'm dead!" he thought. "They didn't even wait for me to wake up. They covered me and left me for dead!" All of a sudden Chauntecleer felt profoundly sorry for Chauntecleer.

"Well, they rot!" he decided with monumental dignity. "I can do without them," he proclaimed to his soul. "Let them go their selfish ways. Chauntecleer the Rooster was ever the noblest bird of them all!" And speaking that way in his heart, Chauntecleer composed himself for an eternity of lonely suffering.

But the colors around him never ceased pulsing. Slowly they began to move as with a purpose, drawing together, wrapping themselves around a shape. They were taking form. And they were blending into each other—swirling, mixing, losing distinction, until all the colors were one color: dun. And the shape was the shape of a Cow.

Chauntecleer's heart leaped! He blinked and looked very hard.

Yes! He saw the rangy, pointed horns of the Dun Cow and her liquid eyes, so soft with sympathy. They were in pain, these eyes, and the Rooster knew them very well.

"You didn't forget!" Chauntecleer cried—without opening his mouth. "You saw my suffering! They left me, but you, my friend—you came back to me!" The cry caused sparks to fly all around his head, and the image of the Dun Cow wavered, like a water reflection.

But this is the sadness of Chauntecleer's hopeless condition, that wild delight can fall quickly into a wild and bitter tantrum. Nothing lasts.

When the image of the Dun Cow stilled again, anger exploded in Chauntecleer's brains. Her eyes were as sympathetic as before, but now he could see that *they were not looking at him.* There was company between the Dun Cow and himself. Mundo Cani Dog was there. And *him* was the Dun Cow gazing at!

"Out! Out! Out!" roared the Rooster, still without the benefit of his mouth. "My place isn't yours anymore, Dog! Get out of the Coop! Out of the camp! Die, you loathsome—"

But no one seemed to mind his bellowing. Neither the Dun Cow, who had now begun to shape her mouth as if talking; nor the Dog, whose bent head and hanging ears were lost in listening; nor the Hen— The Hen!

"Pertelote! You too?"

Chauntecleer was sick.

The two who had been closest to him, whom he had loved most deeply, these had stolen from him the warm attention and the healing gaze of the Dun Cow! *They* were the chief conspirators! Having taken his life—covering and leaving him to die—now they were burying him, cutting him off from the one being who could give him life again. So the Dun Cow would feed a filthy Dog, while a Rooster perished. And a Hen could watch the murder without guilt!

"Now I know, Pertelote! Now I know there's nothing left for me!" Chauntecleer's sorrow on his own behalf was immeasurable.

But the next thing that he saw silenced and confused him.

Obeying some direction from within her, the Dun

[212]

Cow stepped back from the Dog. As she did, her gaze for him grew more and more anguished. Her very eyes began to melt for grief, and her face contorted in an agony. "Oooo, Mundo Cani," she groaned in a wonderful voice.

It was clear that she was suffering, and that for the Dog. But he remained still and bowed, listening, listening.

"Oooo, Mundo Cani," again in that terrible moan.

Suddenly she swung round to the wall of the Coop, closed her eyes, and cracked her head against the wooden beams, all in one hard motion. Not her head— her *horn*! Again and again she hit the wood with the side of her horn, bunching the muscles in her neck, throwing the entire weight of her body behind each blow, weeping. Again and again the Coop shook under the assault. Then a splitting sound shivered the air, a cry of pain: The horn broke off at the skull, and fell to the ground like lumber.

Neither Mundo Cani nor Pertelote had moved an inch. It was as if the Dun Cow were still speaking quietly at their ears. But she wasn't. From the door of the Coop she was regarding the Dog with an inexpressible sorrow. She had but one horn remaining, for the other she had left behind. The Cow had become a cripple.

Then, just before she turned to walk away, she raised her eyes and looked directly at Chauntecleer.

"Modicae fidei," she said in the hidden language, but the Rooster heard her with absolute clarity; her voice was like a waterfall. *"Quare dubitasti?* Chauntecleer, Chauntecleer! Don't you know yet that it is all for you? Ah, no, and you will not know till done is done for good."

The look and the language pierced him utterly. He woke up.

The colors, the death pall, the self-pity, the vicious conspiracy against him, the Dun Cow and her final glance—all whirled in the Rooster's brains, together with the outrageous pain of his body.

"Who are you?" he said to the air, because the Dun Cow was truly gone. This time he used his mouth for the question, and a pale, stupid voice—but a real one—came out.

"Maybe this, maybe that." Mundo Cani answered the question as he stood beside Chauntecleer's bed. "Me the Rooster used to know. My back he used to stand on when he crowed the morning in. But a back may change, God knows. And a Dog who was this yesterday may be that today."

How long had the Dog been pattering this useless speech, word after mumbled, meaningless word? It seemed to Chauntecleer that it had been a very long time.

"After what he has done to Cockatrice, after that victory, should I be surprised if the Rooster doesn't know who I am?"

Painfully Chauntecleer turned his head away from the Coop wall. He perceived a nose—and instantly he hated that nose more than anything else in the whole world. It was the nose on the face of failure. Not the cause, but the symbol of their hopeless predicament. And it was worn by one who could betray!

"Filthy—mongrel," Chauntecleer groaned in a metal voice. "Deserted—me."

"The Rooster—" Mundo Cani said, new light flashing in his eyes, his throat swallowing again and again, the whole Dog trying hard not to weep. "My Rooster! You are alive! You're talking!"

"I—disown—you," Chauntecleer rasped, focusing on the nose and trembling that it should be so close to him. "I never—knew—you."

"Oh, glory be!" Mundo Cani cried. He backed away a step and broke into a little dance. "Glory be to God! Master of the Universe, he lives!"

"Fool!" Chauntecleer shouted, and the pain of that shout nearly split his being into two. "Get," he whispered, glaring like Cockatrice himself, "out of my—sight."

Then Mundo Cani did leave him, and Chauntecleer counted that a tiny victory. With all his heart he desired that Mundo Cani should hurt, should feel a guilt more intense than the Dog had ever felt before. Oh, that nose was a vile thing!

But it was a passing victory. The nose was back in a second, bouncing its jubilation and bringing Pertelote behind.

"Words he spoke to me," the Dog explained.

The Hen came very close to Chauntecleer and searched him gently for his wounds. Chauntecleer tried to pull back from her and failed. He could not command his broken body anymore. Helpless!

"You," he leered at the Hen, "and the Dun Cow, what?" He made a ghastly attempt at a nod, an accusing nod. "A Dog and a Hen. So. And the Dun Cow. So. I know. I know. You are against me."

"Things and stuff, Pertelote," Mundo Cani said, sympathy and joy stuck together in his throat. "The poor Rooster wanders in his brains. Confused he has a right to be after such a struggle with Cockatrice."

Chauntecleer blazed with anger. Stars burst in his head, and he nearly passed out again from the pain.

But Pertelote ignored Mundo Cani's explanation and spoke sincerely to Chauntecleer himself. "Who is this Dun Cow?" she asked: "Chauntecleer, what are you trying to tell us? We can't wait much longer to act the final act. The river, Chauntecleer. The river is at the wall of the camp. If you know anything at all, tell us, and help us to understand."

At this new information the Rooster squeezed his eyes shut. The expression on his face jumped and twisted dreadfully. His sad, ragged body began to shake, and a thin hiss escaped his mouth. Chauntecleer had begun to laugh!

[215]

"Then you too—are going—to die," the ruined Rooster giggled. "Justice."

"Chauntecleer!" Pertelote stood back, shocked. "Is that what you have to say to us?"

"He is sick," Mundo Cani said quietly, himself astonished at the depth of the sickness. "He does not know what he says."

Oh, God! Chauntecleer thought to himself. The treachery of that nose! Self-righteous nose!

Aloud he whispered furiously: "I am dying. We are all going to die. You are going to die. There is nothing left to do."

"No!" Mundo Cani cried, suddenly full of authority. "There is still something left to be done."

And Pertelote, too, as if it ought to make a difference to the Rooster, said, "There *is*, Chauntecleer. There is something yet to do."

But Chauntecleer fixed them with his haunted eyes: "Wyrm is at the wall. Cockatrice was nothing. Wyrm is everything. You two—you betrayed me. You made a way for him. Wyrm will win. Now, get away from me—and let me die alone."

Neither Mundo Cani nor Pertelote made an answer to this speech. They stood side by side, in absolute silence, staring at the Rooster; and the Rooster, for his part, met their stare with his own, challenging, threatening, coldly triumphant, gleaming. He had hurt them! He had found the right thing to say. The nose was powerless.

But, whereas they should have bowed their heads and skulked away, leaving him alone, they didn't. A minute. Two. Five, and then ten—they continued to stare at him with an unbroken astonishment. Not as if they were waiting for another word, but rather stunned by the stranger in front of them.

Then tears began to gather in Mundo Cani's eyes, and his gaze grew mortally woeful, grieving. The tears spilled over unnoticed, ran freely down either side of the nose; and Chauntecleer saw that the Dog's eyes were brown, soft, and full of an inexpressible sorrow.

Finally Mundo Cani did bow his head. He said something to Pertelote without looking at her. When she did not move, he used his enormous nose to nudge her gently, push by push, to a far corner in the Coop. Then he walked sadly to the Rooster.

"There is still something left to be done," he said. He opened his mouth, lowered it over Chauntecleer, and lifted the Rooster bodily from his bed, between jaws hard and wet.

Chauntecleer's mind buzzed at Mundo Cani's strange behavior. For one instant he thought he would struggle against the teeth; Gaff and the Slasher were still bound to his spurs. But he was helpless, dying, and the Dog's bite was simply too strong for him. So he gave up. He didn't care. Dying is dying, however it may happen. And if a Dog was soon to crush him body and bones, then he, Chauntecleer, would make the only choice left to him in a hopeless world: He would say nothing. He would die in silence—tragically, but with a hero's dignity.

You see? You see? He thought to himself. I was right. It had to come to this.

But Mundo Cani did not bite him to death on the spot. Neither did he chew the Rooster slowly. Instead, he turned, glanced at Pertelote, then stepped out of the Coop into the white light of the day. Neither did he stop once he was outside.

He began to walk through the camp with the Rooster in his mouth.

[217]

[[TWENTY-SIX]] *Processional*

Well, dying is dying, to be sure; but some dying is more decent and respectable and dignified than other dying. And the farther Mundo Cani carried him through the camp, the more Chauntecleer woke up to the indignity of this kind of dying.

Here were his wings and legs all trussed up in this satchel of a mouth, his head upside down, his comb brushing the dust of the earth! Underneath the greater, more tragic feelings contending in his soul, Chauntecleer began to experience a tiny twinge of irritation: A mouth simply cannot compare to a bed for dying in.

What did the Dog think he was doing after all? What could possibly happen outside that might not be done in the Coop, and done better? Murder knows no place. It doesn't need to be public. Chauntecleer's twinge of irritation turned into positive displeasure; and in spite of his pain he did, now, try to squirm, to stitch Mundo Cani's throat with the point of the Slasher; but the effort was useless. Chauntecleer gave it up and looked around.

Behold! His own animals—the animals for whom he had fought Cockatrice to the death, the animals over whom he was Lord and leader—were lining up on either side of Mundo Cani's progress and were staring at this indignity!

So what did this Dog think he was doing?

At first the animals only looked in wonderment, simply bewildered, not one of them offering assistance to their Lord or the least expression of sympathy. They gaped, and Chauntecleer was stung. He put a noble, wounded look upon his face. What was his death? A show for everybody to see?

[218]

But then Tick-tock the Black Ant popped. Perhaps the long strain of this war had finally affected his manners, his propriety, his soldierly poise. Or maybe the fact that Wyrm and the river were so impossibly close to them all had unloosed his senses. Whatever the reason, when Tick-tock saw this sight he began to giggle a crazy giggle. He didn't mean to. As soon as the giggle had dribbled out, he stooped over and buried his tiny black head in the dirt. But his little body shook, and the giggle came out anyway.

That giggle started things. As if on command, a thousand Black Ants broke ranks and all of them began giggling, too. And then many animals were giggling. They hid their giggles as best they could. They were ashamed of them. But they couldn't help it, and they giggled nonetheless.

Chauntecleer's head, his comb, and his wattles were hanging like baggage out of one side of Mundo Cani's mouth. Out of the other side there stuck his proud flag of a tail. And Mundo Cani held his own head, with all its ornaments, very high.

Now, a giggle is only the promise of things to come. It is the weakness in a strong defense; and once this weakness has been found, the rest of the attack is sure to follow. The animals were attacked. All in spite of themselves, shaking their heads and full of guilt at what they were doing, they exploded. They burst out laughing.

Chauntecleer wasn't displeased anymore. He was mortified.

"You sack!" he cried; and the pain which stabbed him from that cry assured him that this ridiculous ride was not a dream.

But Mundo Cani took no notice—either of the Rooster's rage or of the insane laughter all around him. He continued to walk steadily toward the wall.

"What the devil is the matter with you?" Chauntecleer roared from his upside-down head. "I told *you* to get away! Not to take *me* away!" Then he coughed.

The more the Rooster cared about his humiliation, the less he cared about his pain. Oh, he would endure the pain, if only he could get three bloody-honest swear words in at this outrageous mongrel!

Animals were falling down all around him, helpless in their laughter. Weasels rolled and pounded the ground. Otters slithered on their backs, kicking the air and holding their sides. Sheep sniggered out of the corners of their mouths. Pigs lowered their eyes and burped offensively. The Ducks and the Geese set up an infuriating beeping, and even the Hens—lo, the Hens! The Hens cackled like stuffed nincompoops!

The whole camp dithered and giggled, shouted, roared, snorted, and *laughed*. And they weren't ashamed of it anymore! At the lip edge of disaster they had all gone mad. And Mundo Cani, his mouth stuffed full of a Rooster, his head high and purposeful, saw nothing of it.

But Chauntecleer—the worse he felt, the better he felt. He prayed earnestly for the chance to kick a certain nose until it swelled as big as a tree. He was ready. By God, he was ready to live again for the sake of revenge!

"Ack! You suitcase! There are *ways* to carry a Lord among his animals!—"

BOOM!

Water surged straight up above the edge of the wall— a wave that hit the sky and then fell back down upon itself.

Chauntecleer's eyes popped open. He was silenced. The animals, too, fell suddenly silent before the enormity of the wave and the nearness of its power.

Only Mundo Cani remained unchanged. Forward toward the wall he walked with the same speed. And when he had reached it, without the least hesitation, he began to climb it.

BOOM!

The belly of the wave was right before Chauntecleer's face. He wanted to lunge backward from the ripping

[220]

water, but he couldn't. Mundo Cani had laid him on the top of the wall, and then had placed a paw on top of him—was looking into his eyes.

"Mundo Cani!" Chauntecleer cried. "Look at it!"

The Dog didn't, but the Rooster did. From the trench to the horizon was the river, heaving great gouts of water at the sky. Massive waves rushed out of this sea to the camp and broke themselves against its poor wall. Mountainous, furious waves, foaming in their rage, slammed into the wall, leaped straight toward the sky, hissed and sprayed everywhere, then rained back down as from a storm.

The animals huddled in the center of the camp. All at once they seemed to be miserably few. But Pertelote had stepped away from them and now was herself approaching the wall.

"Pertelote!" Chauntecleer cried. "You don't want to be here! Get back! Save yourself!"

BOOM!

But neither the wave nor the Rooster's warning turned her around. She began to climb the wall.

"Forgive this Dog," Mundo Cani shouted close to Chauntecleer's ear, "but the Rooster was wrong. He is *not* going to die. There is still something to be done."

Pertelote was with them, now. As if it were her duty, she embraced the Rooster with a strange strength, and the Dog removed his paw.

Chauntecleer's eye rolled back and forth between the sad band within the camp and the spouting black water without. "There is nothing to be done anymore," he said—to himself, for the roaring waters killed his words.

"Something!" Mundo Cani shouted. There was a yearning in his eyes that he be understood. "One thing left to do. I am going away."

"What!" Chauntecleer would have stood up to face the Dog, except that Pertelote's hold restrained him.

[221]

"This Dog must leave now."

Chauntecleer's eyes blazed. "This is an answer?"

"It must be done."

"I *knew* it, you wretch! No dream at all, but the truth I saw—I knew you for a traitor! You wretch! Oh, you wretch! Be gone and be damned, you and your everlasting tumor. It'll do you no good!"

For the second time in a little while, Mundo Cani gazed upon Chauntecleer with a stricken pain. Chauntecleer turned his head away and stared at the heaving sea on the other side of the wall.

BOOM! BOOM! BOOM!

The waves hit the wall in running succession. Something, something soon must break under such an almighty bombardment.

When the Rooster looked back again, the Dog had gone. Pertelote and he were alone on top of the wall.

It was then that the earth opened up.

[222]

[TWENTY-SEVEN] "A Dog with no illusion"—the last battle, the war

"*S*um *Wyrm, sub terra!*" The voice seethed from the raging river. From the ground within the camp (and the animals shrank in terror), from the forest and the land beyond, the voice echoed and reechoed as if the whole earth were a drum thundering. The wall was shaken by the sound: Parts of it cracked, other parts crumbled. It seemed to Chauntecleer that he was hearing the voice through the very trembling beneath his feet.

"*Sum Wyrm, sub terra.* There was a chance once, Chauntecleer; but the chance is no more." This voice was legion—a chorus of voices, a thousand choirs singing all around his head: "*I am Wyrm from underneath the earth, coming, coming! I mean to be free!*"

The little Rooster on the top of the wall and facing the sea, Chauntecleer, in the grip of Pertelote, began to shriek:

"Come, snake! Viper! Come! I don't care! I don't care anymore! This is the way that it ends!"

The shaking of the earth grew more violent. Whole sections of the wall slipped sideways, broke into great, tumbling chunks; and then there were gaps in the wall. A mysterious confusion struck the waves of the sea: Instead of their rhythmic rolling toward the camp, there was a dizzy turning. They slapped and struggled against one another, giants without direction. They came together, these waves, like enormous hands, clapping.

Chauntecleer jerked against Pertelote's hold, writhed in her wings.

"Why not?" he screamed as the breach in the wall came very close to him; soon he and Pertelote were on a narrow pedestal, and nowhere to go. "Why not? This is the way that it should be, Wyrm! It is all falling apart!" In spite of his broken body, he doubled his effort to tear himself out of Pertelote's grip. And he would have slashed her, too, if he could have.

But a ponderous growl ascended from the river—a new sound—and then the very earth sprang back.

Chauntecleer was thunderstruck.

As if the earth had a mouth, as if that mouth were opening in a yawn, a chasm had opened up where once there was a battlefield. The pedestal, the whole camp, moved backward slowly, as if in reverence before this hole, to give it space. Suddenly Chauntecleer and Pertelote were on the edge of an abysmal cliff, while across the chasm the other edge was hidden by the torrents of water falling into it. To the left and to the right, as far as the eye could see, the crack in the earth went away—and the gorge was widening. The mantle of the earth had split!

"Sum Wyrm, sub terra!"

The voice was greater than the roaring of the waterfall—falls that had no ending either east or west: The chasm was drinking the entire sea before it, and the sea rushed into it like suicide. But ever farther the sea and the falls moved away from the Rooster and the Hen beside him: The gorge was widening.

"Coming, coming! I mean to be free!"

Now, for the first time, this great voice had a single source. All in spite of himself Chauntecleer found that he was bending forward to see to the bottom of the chasm. As he did he felt as if he were high in the air and in danger

[224]

for his life. But he looked: It was from *there* that the voice rose up.

"Wyrm," he whispered. But still he saw nothing. He saw the waters cascade and boil at the bottom. He saw the rocky maw of the earth still separating in the deep. He saw mud sliding down the nearer wall and stones spinning past the mud, down and down deeper than he would have believed possible.

Then the very bottom of the gorge convulsed, rumpled—and in a moment the odor of rot burst into Chauntecleer's face. He fell backward. Unconsciously he reached for Pertelote and buried his face in the feathers at her throat. The smell there was good. Pertelote touched him at his shoulder. The Rooster swallowed twice and wept—ashamed.

"No good!" The voice from the pit, frightening in its clarity. *"And late, too late, Chauntecleer! I am coming, coming! I mean to be free!"*

Without releasing Pertelote, Chauntecleer looked down again to the bottom; and he saw Wyrm.

Slowly easing itself between the lower jaws of the pit was a long black body of horrible size. Neither head nor tail, neither beginning nor end could be seen, for they passed miles and miles away through the earth; and the greater bulk of Wyrm's roundness was still lodged yet deeper than the bottom of the pit. But the body was turning like a rolling mill, turning, sloughing huge fields of rotting flesh as it did—and this body, as far away as Chauntecleer could see, was itself the floor of the gorge.

As Wyrm turned, the chasm, the earth crack, grew—a mighty power driving it. And the water, when finally it hit Wyrm's flesh, steamed.

Chauntecleer drew Pertelote to himself and held her in despair.

"The Keepers," Wyrm said, *"have failed. They broke. And the earth is breaking. And I shall be free. And I shall be free!"*

[225]

"God forgive me," Chauntecleer breathed.

Pertelote said, "He will. There is one thing left to do."

"What is left?" said the Rooster in an agony.

But they had to leap backward. They had to race ahead of collapsing ground. Sections of the camp sighed and began to fall into the chasm, down and down the face of it. Earth along the edge of it simply gave up and slid away. The gorge was widening.

"What to do?" cried Chauntecleer, clawing at his breast. For the next thing was that the Coop was on the edge of the precipice. And the next thing was that it, too, leaned drunkenly toward the deep, as if looking. And then the next thing was that its back end lifted off the ground. It hung on the edge a moment, considering its death; then it tipped over and passed away.

"What? Pertelote, what?" Chauntecleer screamed as he ran back to the eating cliff.

A long, long time the Coop spun downward, until it was tiny—until, a leaf, it landed on the floor, Wyrm's flesh, and flashed into flame.

"WYRM!"

Chauntecleer looked up, stared wildly about, to see who had cried out with such a piercing conviction. Who had challenged Wyrm?

The animals were mewling at the edge of the forest, frantic at the disappearance of the ground in front of them, squirming one under the other's belly, making an ingrown knot of themselves—a helpless lot.

"WYRM! Does evil look upon a Dog?"

Not from the animals! But running in a shaggy, loping, easy gait along the very lip of the chasm, never missing a step, staring nose over into the vile depths—Mundo Cani, far, far west of the Rooster!

"Wyrm, look at me! Wyrm, see me! A Dog! A Dog! A nothing to look upon!"

Chauntecleer, too, was on the edge. He saw the body

[226]

cease turning for a little moment. Wyrm, wound through the earth, held still.

"A Dog is going to fight with you!"

Now Chauntecleer shot a narrow look at this Dog. Fight with him! For God's sake, Mundo Cani!

Suddenly, a closer look and recognition: Mundo Cani was carrying a weapon. Wood, it seemed, like any other bleached branch, but curved and dangerously sharp. Or bone brought to a lethal point. Or this: It looked exactly like the lost horn of the Dun Cow!

"Oh, Wyrm! Oh, Wyrm!" Mundo Cani cried—bellowed, challenged in a ringing, imperative bark. So lightly he ran along the wasting cliff, dancing away from the chunks that nodded and tumbled in. Mundo Cani had a talent.

"Oh, Wyrm! Great Wyrm—afraid to look at a nothing, a nose, a flea! Fears to see the speck that calls him out! Such evil, to split the earth, but from a Dog—a Dog to hide! WYRM—" A cry to heaven and earth, a cry to all the regions underneath the earth: "WYRM!"

Chauntecleer cast a quick glance to Pertelote. She had known this! But when he looked at her he saw that she was huddled to the earth, covering her face and her eyes and her ears against Mundo Cani's lonely game.

Chauntecleer's heart split. He began to gather dust and throw it upon himself. The high, thin wail of grief and guilt rose up from his chest and filled the air around him.

"Oh, my God!" he wept.

"Wyrm! Wyrm! Wyrm!" Mundo Cani was sneering, needles he sent with the utmost scorn down into the pit. He was running the edge far, far away from Chauntecleer.

Then the body below began to move again. Not turning, this time, but with a new purpose it slid straight in the crevice: bunching and sliding, bunching and sliding.

"A Dog is going to fight with you! It is right! Of all the noble, a Dog is chosen. Look at me, Wyrm—and see your-

[227]

self, evil Wyrm!" Mundo Cani swung the horn in wild arcs. "But look! Look! Oh, Wyrm, look at me!"

Then deep in the gorge, sliding out of the stone, out of the dungeons of the earth, there came a single, steady eye.

Monstrous, unblinking, lidless and looking, that cold eye, Wyrm's eye. White around black, and black so black that all the hosts of night might enter there and never be found again.

Mundo Cani had his wish. Wyrm was looking at him.

For one second Mundo Cani crouched, taut upon the cliff, the long horn between his teeth. Then, with a cry, he leaped.

Over the edge, past the mud, missing the rock like a shadow, down and down Mundo Cani fell, the white horn livid in the dark.

The eye had almost begun to turn. But Mundo Cani had aimed himself well, had made an arrow of his fall. He hit the eye hard, with all four feet. He scrambled, grabbed a footing with his sharp claws, raised the horn, and drove it to the butt through the white flesh.

How Wyrm raged then!

Back and forth the body slammed against the sides of the canyon, the earth crack. Howlings ascended, as if the caverns of the earth were all Wyrm's throat, all filled with his hideous dismay. No longer was his vast motion controlled. It was mad, enraged—and blind.

The far side of the chasm began to crumble altogether. Boulders hurtled into the deep. The streaming water gouged and pounded the cliff face, digging at the weaker parts, spitting out stone, and raking the face to the bottom of it. Soon rock and the whole wall burst inward, spraying and then jamming the bottom. The sea above simply stumbled, as if surprised in its forward walk by a drop-off: The sea stumbled, then settled much lower than it was before. And in a moment—by rock and boulders, by mud and mountains of loose earth; and by the mixing water, a strong mortar—the chasm was filled, the earth crack patched.

In heaven the clouds ripped asunder like a veil. And the light of the sun plunged down and filled the earth. And Chauntecleer could see. And Chauntecleer, in a world suddenly silent, suddenly bright, grieved.

Behind him neither Coop nor camp nor wall. A desolation.

In front of him, at a good distance from him, a sparkling and peaceful sea. And, finally, between him and the sea, an endless scar east to west in the face of the earth—an angry seam closed.

It was this scar that the little Rooster was watching. But he wasn't seeing the scar at all. Over and over again in his mind—as if it were still happening—he was watching a memory: He remembered that as Wyrm swung himself about so grimly a moment ago, and as the wall was caving in on him, there was a Dog in his eye, stabbing and stabbing that eye with a long horn until the eye was no more than a blind and shredded socket.

Wyrm, and more than Wyrm—that scar had knit Mundo Cani into the earth.

In sunshine Chauntecleer went to Pertelote and lay down next to her.

"Marooned," he said. He buried his face in the flaming feathers of her throat. "Marooned."

Here ends the third part of the story about Wyrm's campaign for freedom, its failure, and a Dog's curious entrance into the Netherworld.

FINAL WORD

[TWENTY-EIGHT] *And the last thing done is Pertelote's doing*

ohn Wesley Weasel did not die; but it took him a long time to accept that fact.

More than ever before in his life he developed an abhorrence for the light. It made him sick, both in body and soul, just by being light when he should have awoken in death's darkness. It hurt his eyes, since he was, after all, a Weasel and every Weasel weakness about him was intensified during his convalescence. It humiliated him, for he would catch other animals flitting odd glances at his one-eared head and at the hairless scar along his side. It angered him: The sun had never—never once—shone upon the Wee Widow Mouse when she was alive with him; but now that she was dead, and now that the sun had no business being, it shone with an outrageous glory. For John Wesley Weasel, sunshine now was a cruel gift, come altogether too late.

So as soon as he could walk he took himself into the darkness. There was no Coop for the shade, no roof for the covering, no floor nor any space beneath a floor for the hiding. He went back to his burrow at the base of a certain maple tree.

"Is no use in it," he said, and he determined never again to come out.

Pertelote heard these remarks. She had been tending to the Weasel all through his healing.

"Mice cleans in the spring. What's that to kill for and to take a house away?"

When, after several days and nights, he neither came out of his burrow nor made a sound inside of it, Pertelote took the problem to Chauntecleer—who dealt with it directly.

"Yo, John!" He set up a clamor from the middle of the flat, empty yard. "John, yo! Wesley, yo! Weasel!"

The rest of the animals he had sent to their homes. Scattered about him, pecking and working with an afternoon's industry (for it *was* the middle of the afternoon, and the proper canonical crow *had* been crowed as ever it was before the violation of the times by Wyrm) were twenty-nine dutiful Hens, while seven adolescent Mice buzzed between the yard and the forest, a-gathering.

There came no answer from the burrow.

"John Wesley, laggard! Get out of there! We are not going to bring you food. We are not going to spend pity on you. And when you have wasted away we are not going to mourn a fool's passing. Get out and get to work! There's work to be done in this place!"

Work, indeed. A sea to the south of them. A little closer than the sea, the scar, which had never yet grown a single blade of grass in its clenched, poisonous soil. And then, from the scar to the forest, an open space which had once been the busy center of Chauntecleer's land and the Coop—but was now mere open space.

"It's done, John Wesley; and now the time is ours again, if we make it so. It's done, John Wesley! And now we look to the day. We put it back together again."

But still, from the burrow beneath the maple, nothing.

"Okay, that's it, Pertelote," Chauntecleer said to the Hen, turning his back to the forest. "I've no time for a mope."

"But it will kill him."

"That's what he wants, isn't it?"

"Is that what you want?"

"Want! I want my land made new again. I want the past

[234]

scrubbed out of my soul. I want never to think of it again."

"You can't help thinking about it," Pertelote said. "And you are not, Chauntecleer, able to clean out of your soul the thing that has changed you. Do pity the Weasel. He's slower with the changes than you are. He needed the past and its order more than you, for all of his bluster."

"As long as he remembers in this way, as long as he sulks, he's a memory for *me* of what happened. I'm going to forget the past, Pertelote. And if I have to forget John Wesley with it—well, so. That's the way it is."

"And Mundo Cani?"

"What"—Chauntecleer bristled—"*about* Mundo Cani?"

"Then you forget him, too?"

"No!"

But, yes. As a matter of fact, ever since the war was done and the earth closed, Chauntecleer had wanted to forget Mundo Cani, because there was guilt in such a memory. The Dog's good act stood ever in accusation of the Rooster's sinfulness. Chauntecleer did not like to think of himself as a failure at the final moment. Therefore Chauntecleer did not like to think of Mundo Cani at all.

And that, strangely, is why he was willing to talk about Mundo Cani to anyone and to praise him vigorously.

So Pertelote had not one problem, but two: one whose present was too much steeped in the past, and one whose present denied the past altogether. But the Hen of the crimson throat was equal to both of them. And what she did about them we might call the last and the best battle of all. She talked.

Chauntecleer had a dread of the Netherworld Scar; he was never at ease sleeping on ground level with it. Therefore Pertelote had not the least trouble talking the Rooster into a roost above ground. That she chose for the roost a certain maple tree at the edge of the forest was of little consequence to the Rooster. Its branches were lean, clean, and low for the leap; twenty-nine-plus-one Hens and a Rooster could be well accomodated by the maple; so to the maple they repaired for the night.

There Chauntecleer crowed both vespers and compline. And thence the Hens pattered the ground below. That is to say, they flipped their tail feathers, they delivered a damp *plop* to the ground, and they snugly resettled themselves on the branch above. That is to say, they relieved themselves there. It was a most natural performance for the Hens. They had done it all their lives. The only difference was that now they were dropping their wet packages around, near, and into John Wesley's burrow. This made for discomfort and for a very sour sulk.

Who knew but Pertelote about John Wesley's new distress? Not Chauntecleer. He had gone to sleep. There was much work to do in the morning.

Therefore Pertelote woke him up.

"Mundo Cani!" she said loudly—angrily, in fact.

"What?"

"Mundo Cani Dog. Nothing more. Good night."

But, of course, she had made the night instantly ungood, and Chauntecleer could not go back to sleep. Pertelote's tone had been curt, forbidding; so he didn't feel that he should talk, either. What was left? He tried twelve various positions, shaking the limb heartily with each one and giving Pertelote herself something to think about.

Finally he burst out: "Mundo Cani *what?*"

A Weasel below tried to turn his wrinkled snout from the entrance to the shaft of his burrow and failed.

"He's on your mind," she snapped.

"He is not!"

"No, of course he isn't."

"He is, too!"

"Of course he is."

"I haven't forgotten him, Pertelote, if that's what you mean."

"Nothing of the kind. You memorialize him."

[236]

"But I don't dwell on him, if that's what you mean."

"Ah, no. The past is past."

"Right!"

For a second Chauntecleer felt satisfied that he had won the argument. Then he lost confidence and wasn't so sure anymore, wasn't even sure what the argument had been about. Something, it seemed, was bothering Pertelote. But she had been a patient saint ever since the disappearance of the Dog; so it was a sudden something. The Dog. In a rush the memory of Mundo Cani filled Chauntecleer's mind, and he was humbled.

"Pertelote?"

"What?"

"I miss him." Chauntecleer was speaking the truth. "Oh, Pertelote, I miss him terribly."

"I know that, Chauntecleer."

All at once her voice was gentle and comforting. Yet she said no more than that. Much more than that she wanted to hear from the Rooster, so she was letting his thoughts work inside him for a while.

Chauntecleer was wide awake, now; and Mundo Cani was a living, eating thing in his soul. Again and again against the night he saw the Dog raising the horn over Wyrm's eye to plunge it in. Again and again, in rhythm, he heard the last words of the Dun Cow: *Modicae fidei—it is all for you.*

Finally: "That should have been *me*," he said. "I should have gone down into the pit, not Mundo Cani. I should have died instead of him."

"So," Pertelote said. Then she probed deeper—still gently, but with a cold pressure: "And what else?"

"Why, I am the leader. It was my duty to see such a thing and to do it, not the Dog's. This is not right. Today is wrong; tonight, *now* is wrong! I'm living a stupid, extended existence. I have no right to this life. It's his. It's Mundo Cani's!"

"And that's why you work so hard during the day."

"Oh, I don't know."

"To busy yourself. To pay him back by breaking yourself. That's one thing. But what else, Chauntecleer?"

"What else? There is nothing else. A leader lost and a Dog took over. A leader lived to be sick of his life. You've heard it. What do you mean, 'What else'?"

"What else do you owe Mundo Cani?"

"My life! Dammit, Pertelote—what else is there to give?"

"Penance."

"What?"

"Penance. It is more than your life. It is that scrubbing of the past which you want so much, because it is confession. It is the new birth of the present, which you want so much, because it prepares for deliverance. The one is separated from the other by forgiveness. It is the honoring, Chauntecleer, of the worth in *his* life. Penance. You can tell him you are sorry. He will forgive you."

"For what! He went down and it should have been me. So! I've said so. For what else?"

"Oh, Chauntecleer. He *knew* he had to go down. Don't you understand that? There was never any question about who would make the sacrifice. Leader or not, it just wasn't your place to go. Cockatrice was yours; but Wyrm's eye was his. So it was from the beginning. So it had to be. And so he told me when you were raving in the Coop strange things about a Cow. With neither fear nor hesitation he told me this thing, the last thing left to do. He accepted it as destiny. This is not your sin, Proud Chauntecleer; and if you keep saying that it is, you protect yourself against the greater. You are blinding yourself. Penance for what else?"

"Pertelote," Chauntecleer said. "Stop."

"Say it!"

"I can't."

"You know it?"

[238]

"Yes."

"Then *say it!*"

Chauntecleer shivered all over as the thing pushed its way into his throat. He could say it, perhaps, into a hole in the ground. He could give it word, perhaps, when no one else was around. But to say it to Pertelote—his wife, the one who spoke with Mundo Cani when no one else was speaking to him, and when Chauntecleer himself—

"I despised him," Chauntecleer said.

"So," said Pertelote. "This was your wickedness."

"He was making ready to die for us, and I didn't understand that. I judged him a traitor. I made his last moments lonely, and I despised him."

"Did you think that this was a secret, that you should hide it so long?"

"No."

"But this, Chauntecleer—this is your sin?"

"Yes."

The Rooster was very meek right now. And a Weasel below these two had developed, in the recent minutes, a very big ear.

"But now you have said it," Pertelote said, "and that is good. That is the beginning of your life now, because it is the ending of something. Chauntecleer, maybe one day you will say the same to Mundo Cani, and then he will be able to speak his forgiveness in your hearing, and that will complete the matter. Then you will be free of it. Chauntecleer," she said full quietly on the maple limb. She waited until his attention had been turned from his sin unto her. "I love you."

"Thank you," he said foolishly.

Something else was trying to click in his mind. Something she had said, not quite right or real.

"Whoa! *Say* it to Mundo Cani? Pertelote, are you crazy? I saw him closed up underneath the earth!"

[239]

"He was that. Mundo Cani was closed deep in the earth. The Netherworld Scar is a fearsome closing."

"So then the poor Dog is dead."

"No, he is alive. Under the earth, but alive. Dreadfully close to Wyrm, but alive. There was much Mundo Cani told me while you lay in your darkness and would not listen to him. He had a nose for intuition. He is alive, and only the bravest will go to him. Only the bravest will see him again. Perhaps you will, Chauntecleer. I doubt, though, that John Wesley Weasel will have the opportunity—"

"What?" This little word from the smelly burrow below.

"—because that one has given up."

"What?"

"He has gone into a little hole. He will never find the larger one from there, the hole that goes down to the Dog. But I understand that a Weasel who has lost an ear should mourn his loss and feel an invalid thereafter."

"What?"

"There are no more adventures, and very little courage left, for a Weasel with half a head. Surely, there is no use in it if an ear is gone—"

"Double-u's is not Double-u's on account of their ears. Is a Mouse John mourns, you cut-cackle! John can go to the Netherworld as any Rooster can—and he a sinner. Ha! And ha, ha! to you!"

"Because Mundo Cani was never anything to John Wesley but a carriage to carry him about. No friendship—"

"Ha!" cried the Weasel. "Ha, ha, ha! How about *that*?"

"One more 'Ha,' John," Chauntecleer began to shout at him, "and I'll have your other ear for my pocketbook!"

"A Weasel is a Dog's friend, too! Is more love in a Weasel than in a Rooster—proud, silly bird!" John Wesley was fully out of his burrow, now, and bounding around the base of the maple tree, while Chauntecleer leaned dangerously forward to spit his opinions at the Weasel.

"You lost no love for him when he saved you from Cockatrice," roared the Rooster, "when he carried you in his mouth then. I saw. And I didn't hear a 'Thank you' come out of your mouth then, John Wesley Weasel."

"Speaks a Rooster, ha! A Rooster once in the Dog's mouth, too, ha! Ha, ha, to you, Rooster! Is Double-u's what dig; but Roosters only flutter-gut about. Go find the Netherworld without a digger Double-u!"

"Just wait, you slow mope. I'll see that Dog before you do. I'll find the hole into Wyrm's caverns before you scratch surface!"

"Ha!"

As it happened, then, Pertelote fell asleep before either of these adversaries did. Far into the night they held lively conversation with one another, pointing out absurdities in each other's character and promising mighty promises, each to be fulfilled at an early date.

But the sound of their brave chatter was good in Pertelote's ears. She had been successful. She slept peacefully.

Here ends the twenty-eighth and final chapter of the story about Chauntecleer and the keeping of Wyrm.